# Chasing the Green Man

# Chasing the Green Man

45 Miles of Mud, Snow, Floods and Frozen Toes!

Richard Meston

Copyright © 2025 by Richard Meston

All rights reserved. No part of this book may be reproduced or used in any manner without the written permission of the copyright owner except for the use of short quotations in a book review.

First paperback edition January 2025

**(Amazon) ISBN: 979-8-3073-3831-5**

Independently published

Also by Richard Meston

*Books in the South West Coast Path Series:*

*Half the Path*
Minehead to Penzance in 9 days. Via the pub.

*Buckle Up*
The five-year journey to the end of a 100-mile foot race.

*Flippin' Hell!*
The seed was sown 14 years ago… now it's time to run 84 miles across 185 million years of coastline.

*Buckle Down*
Hartland Quay to Minehead.
One hundred and ten miles, two feet, one path.

*Running with Dinosaurs*
The Jurassic Coast? Completed it, mate.

*To Harry.*

*Your brain works in mysterious ways,*
*A quandary, an enigma.*
*Locked onto something and not letting go,*
*Both a blessing and a curse.*

*It's a joy to watch you learn and flourish,*
*With those ideas you've got,*
*"This time next year, you'll be a millionaire!"*

*Keep smashing it!*

# Acknowledgements

An endeavour like this is never just the effort of one person, and it would be remiss of me not to mention a few people.

Thanks to Stuart Webster for taking the time to proofread the manuscript, and also in advance for joining me in the 2025 Green Man Ultra (so he can demonstrate how to run it properly!).

There wouldn't *be* a race without Ultrarunning Limited, so a massive thanks to Steve Worrallo and his team for putting on the race for more than the last decade (and producing top class medals!). Thanks also to each and every one of the volunteers all through the course - you guys make it fun (at least as much as it can be), safe and exciting.

Finally, thank you to my family for not only putting up with me running so much throughout the weeks, but then disappearing off for races, and afterwards sitting on the sofa ignoring everyone while I write a bloody book about them! My legs will probably drop off one day, then you'll be fed up with me being around all the time!

# Contents

Preface ..................................................................................... i

Introduction ............................................................................ iii

1 ............................................................................................. 1

2 ............................................................................................. 1

3 ............................................................................................. 6

4 ........................................................................................... 14

5 ........................................................................................... 24

6 ........................................................................................... 32

7 ........................................................................................... 42

8 ........................................................................................... 46

9 ........................................................................................... 52

10 ......................................................................................... 63

11 ......................................................................................... 73

12 ......................................................................................... 90

13 ......................................................................................... 94

# PREFACE

Hello, and welcome to my book about the Green Man Ultra, or specifically my time running said ultramarathon in March 2024.

It was never my intention to write a book, but I seem to have accidentally got into the habit of filling up pages after each adventure I do since attempting to walk the South West Coast Path back in 2021. I found a deep catharsis in the writing and have since got a bit carried away - this is my 8th book, which is a bit bonkers! It's also the first to break the trend of writing about walks or races on the South West Coast Path.

The Green Man was my first ever ultramarathon back in 2014, and in 2024 I ran it for the 5th time. My terrible memory and even worse sense of directions has meant that each time has been like a new race, although with progressively more familiar bits as the years go by. It's a lovely race – well supported by runners and crew alike, a diverse and interesting route but tougher than you might expect given the elevation and terrain (and tougher still if you add in snow and floods!).

If you've read any of my previous books, you'll know roughly what you're in for – lots of route detail, a valiant attempt at humour with the occasional bit of fruity language, and the words wandering off on quite a few tangents, especially when it comes to historical things.

The race in 2024 was an interesting one, so much so that the results page on the website states "Conditions were the toughest yet and huge congratulations to all of the finishers". I hope you enjoy my story about a little jog along the Community Forest Path around Bristol, and that it maybe gets you thinking about giving the Green Man Ultra a go!

*Rich Meston, January 2025*

# INTRODUCTION

Do you know what a Woodwose is? I didn't until sometime in 2013, after I'd spent time devouring every detail on the *Ultrarunning Limited* website about the Green Man Ultra, the one I had picked to pop my ultra cherry, so to speak. Far more than just a race, it embraces a fascinating part of European folklore.

The Green Man is a symbol of nature's regenerative power and is oftentimes shown as a face surrounded or made from leaves and foliage. The image appears throughout history, especially in medieval church carvings and architecture, and is thought to represent the cycle of growth each spring and the connection between humanity and nature.

So, what about a Woodwose? Well, from the race website: "Woodwose is the proper name for the wild men and wild women that haunted the imaginary forests of medieval Europe and is entirely appropriate for anyone mad enough to conquer the Community Forest Path." They're often depicted as hairy, wild figures living in the wilderness – add muddy into that, and you've probably nailed a good percentage of the finishers of the race!

Complete the Green Man Challenge – the 45-mile circumnavigation of Bristol on the Community Forest Path – and you will officially become a Woodwose! You get a certificate signed by The Gaveller and your name added to the rather epic sounding *Forestal Book of the Honourable Order of Woodwoses*.

*Ultrarunning Limited* introduced the ultramarathon and gave some more structure to the Green Man Challenge, bringing a bunch of people along on the same day and supporting them with checkpoints on the 45-mile route. In 2016, the 30-mile route was added starting at Keynsham - checkpoint 2 in the 45-mile race. And in 2019, the race name was changed to the Winter Green Man Ultra to make way for a Summer Green Man Ultra, run in the heat of August instead of the mud of March.

I ran the Green Man Ultra as my first ever ultramarathon back in 2014, taking 11-and-a-half hours to cover 45 miles. The time was irrelevant – I had an amazing day, met some amazing people and – despite having no real idea what the hell I was doing – did an amazing thing.

In 2015, I ran the race again and, having figured out a little more about running, knocked just over 2-and-a-half hours off the time. Lesson very much not learnt, I came back in 2017 with my mate Rob and knocked another 8 minutes off that time.

Over the second half of the decade, I thoroughly enjoyed building up my ultramarathon distance. In 2016, I tackled my first 100 miler – the Centurion Thames Path 100 – and then a second in 2017 with the South Down's Way 100. Both went well – sub-24-hour finishes, which was the target. I started on my journey with the Arc of Attrition (100 miles on the Cornish coast path in the depths of winter!), taking a few attempts to get that one done. While trying to figure out how to not get broken doing the Arc, I knocked out a little 145-mile run from Bristol to London called the Kennet & Avon Canal Race, managing to bag 6th place and get a Spartathlon qualifying time (which I didn't take up, incidentally).

Because the Green Man is such a nice race, I entered in 2020, but this pesky virus thing did the rounds and buggered things up for a couple of years. In 2022, I got an email late in February reminding me I had a place for the race. I had completely forgotten I'd entered over two years before, and that email came with 6 days' notice! Having finally completed the Arc of Attrition less than a month before, I figured I had the fitness and decided I'd drive up, do the race, and drive back in the same day. It worked out okay – sneaking through in just under 9 hours on short notice and with a 90-mile drive each side.

So now you know what a Woodwose is, and you know a little about the history of the race, and my history of running it.

Time to get on with the story…

# 1

### *b82rez*

I drink a lot of coffee. I'm a software engineer, so it's kind-of part of the job description, but I've run quite a few through-the-night ultramarathons where I've found that cutting back the caffeine intake for a few weeks before a race has given me the excitement of night-time superpowers for a few hours.

The problem with the Green Man Ultra is that it's *only* 45 miles (or thereabouts), and it's all done quite cleanly within a single day, which is something I'm not really used to. You think maybe I would be, as this book is all about the fifth time I've run the bloody thing.

Back to caffeine. I couldn't quite work out whether to bother cutting back for a race that didn't go through the night, but I thought that at some point I might come across a particularly shit moment that a good kick up the arse from a cup of chemical stimulant might help, so I resolved to cut back to just one cup a day for the week prior to the race. Not much of an effort, but something.

I have a bit of a routine of eating low carb for a chunk of time before long races. I've listened to a lot of podcasts and that essentially makes me an expert[1], and all my degree-level podcast-consumption had led me to believe that cutting carbs for a few days before a race would kick my body into fat-burning mode, meaning I wouldn't have to eat as much during the race. It's been useful, as despite running ultramarathons for over 10 years now, I've never really figured out a decent in-race nutrition strategy. Like with the caffeine, I made a token effort to drop carbs for 5 of the 7 days before the race, although it was really an attempt at kick-starting lower carb eating through to the 105-mile race I had in June.

Training wise, I didn't really make much of an effort. I wasn't feeling particularly motivated in the 3 months before the race, and my weekly mileage dropped from 40 miles in December, through 35 in January and down to just 30 miles per week in February. I hadn't really been noticing though, under the illusion that I had enough base fitness and experience to do a race like the Green Man without making any real effort to train. Which was a mistake.

The only other real preparation I'd done for this race was to make up a little timing chart, something I've done for the last few ultras so I can keep an eye on how I'm doing in relation to various targets. I had no real idea how I was going to do this year, but I figured I might as well set a PB target, so I opted for 8 hours 30 minutes and worked out times for the top of Dundry Hill, all the checkpoints, and a couple of motorway crossings that would be easy points to spot as I was running.

---

[1] My sister is a biochemist and lipidologist. She has 3 degrees and is a hospital consultant. But she hasn't listened to the podcasts I have, so she doesn't really know all the important stuffs, so I ignore her when she tells me I'm a bit of a plonker.

On the basis that I hadn't really done any sensible training, I also opted to add a few more columns to the chart. I put on my times for 2017 (my PB year, with a finish time of 8 hours 42 minutes) and 2022 where I finished in just under 9 hours. I figured that would be the worst case – 3 out of the last 4 times I'd run the race was under 9 hours, and the first time didn't count as it was my first ultra.

I printed out a couple of copies, laminated them with Sellotape in case it rained and stuck one in the back of my pack, with the other going in an easy access front pocket of the vest.

The Green Man takes place on a Saturday, which is a good day of the week as most people aren't doing anything particularly useful.

On the evening of Friday the 1st of March 2024, I was sat on the sofa watching the rather ~~excellent~~ ridiculous film that is "Ali G Indahouse" with my 15-year-old son, something he'd been looking forward to being old enough to witness. I was aiming to be in bed by 8pm, but things ran on and I didn't want Oz to miss the "b82rez 2g4"[2] smoky-laser-dancing scene so it was about 9pm when I finally pulled the duvet up and turned the light off.

I stuck on the BBC Sounds Friday Night Comedy podcast of the *News Quiz*, sure I'd be asleep in minutes. After finishing the *News Quiz*, I stuck on *Inside Science*, and half an hour later, *The Infinite Monkey Cage*. I was not falling asleep, which was making me frustrated.

---

[2] B8-2-rez... Bat-2-rez... *batteries*. 2g4... 2-ge-four... *together*. Obvious when you know. Makes no sense? – watch the film!

I kept putting new programs on, and I must have slept for chunks because there were lots of the latter halves of things that I didn't remember, but I was certainly not getting decent chunks of sleep through that night. It was definitely not the sort of interrupted rest you want before a big day out.

# 2

*Whatever fine mess I'd got myself into*

## Saturday 2nd March 2024, 04:00

When my watch alarm blasted out it's shrill, vibrating call, I woke immediately and silenced it so as not to wake Eva, my wife. It took a further minute before I realised I was alone in the bed.

Eva had been working until 11pm on that Friday, and it was her first day back at work since breaking her ankle back in early November. I checked my phone and saw that she had arrived back last night, so figured she had decided to sleep upstairs (our house is upside down) so as not to disturb my sleep. Little did she know it wouldn't have made much difference at all.

With no-one else in the room to disturb, I clicked on the bedside light and lay in bed for a minute, checking my phone. My mate Mark Smith had sent a few messages taking the piss and generally ribbing me about what I had in store, and a check of the weather showed light snow in Bristol in a few hours. I dismissed it – living on the south coast of England, we rarely get snow, so whenever I see the weather forecast mentioning snow, I just assume it means "somewhere else". I had completely forgotten that, today, I was *going* "somewhere else".

With Eva not being in the room, I figured I could make a bit of a racket getting ready, so I turned on all the lights to try and wake myself up and headed to the bathroom. I had a wash, then tipped out the bag I'd prepared the night before with everything I needed carefully arranged.

Five minutes later, I was dressed in my Decathlon undercrackers, new softer and warmer compression shorts and long tights with a pair of light shorts over the top. I rarely wear long tights for running – usually only for the Arc of Attrition which has a mandatory requirement for either wearing or carrying long trousers (and I wasn't going to carry them!) – but I had a feeling today was going to be cold.

I had on a green compression t-shirt, and a black merino wool long-sleeved top on top of that. At the very bottom of my legs, I had on my trusty Montane Via gaiters, a pair of Injinji toe-socks and a pair of Drymax socks on top of that. It was going to be wet, and it was going to be muddy, so a double layer of socks seemed like a sensible idea.

I grabbed my hat from the radiator that I'd washed the previous night and packed a couple of other things back in the bag, like compression calf guards and a pair of shorts, just in case I arrived in Bristol and the weather turned out to be tropical.

Upstairs in our silly upside-down house, I snuck into the kitchen and hit the button on the coffee grinder to smash out enough powder to make an Americano to take with me. The noise woke pretty much everyone within a 12-mile radius, including my wife who had been asleep in the lounge. I poured the caffeinated Americano into a travel flask and knocked up a decaf instant coffee to drink now – no sense in waking myself up too much for the 90-mile drive.

I went into the lounge to say hi to Eva and we had a brief chat. Her evening back at work had gone well, but she had slept upstairs so as not to disturb me. Don't feel too bad for her – it was really all part of her cunning plan to end up lying on a sofa at 4 o'clock in the morning covered in cats and dogs, a plan which had worked perfectly!

In a change from the usual race-day routine (which typically involved not eating anything until an hour into the race), I stuffed a chocolate twist into my face. Let's find out if eating carbs early actually helps.

Out in the hallway, I opened the shoe cupboard and took out a carrier bag which contained every I would need for the run. I'd prepared everything last night, to the point of loading my vest up with water bottles so I could be nice and quiet in the morning.

At the bottom of the bag were the clothes I'd worn yesterday – trousers, socks etc. I'd wear those home after the race, and there was no point in putting anything clean on when I'd be covered in 45 miles worth of sweat and Bristol Community Forest Path mud. I stuck in a pair of old comfortable trainers that I could stick on my feet to replace what was likely to be a very muddy and wet pair of running shoes.

My race vest was on top, loaded with all sorts of exciting things. My favourite Rab Powerstrech gloves were in a dog-poo bag (cheap, waterproof and handy, right?) in one side of the front of the vest. The other side had a zip pocket which contained 4 Performance Fuel chews, an SiS chocolate fudge flapjack, my little printed timing chart, and my Bluetooth headphones stuffed in another poo bag to keep them dry in case it rained.

In the back stretch pocket was my Montane Spine jacket and a drybag containing emergency "wet or cold" stuff – waterproof shorts, lightweight waterproof mitts and a warm hat. I'd also stuck in a collapsible cup so I could be all sorts of environmentally friendly, should it be required.

Inside the main section of the pack was my shit kit (very, very unlikely to be required, but if it was, it would be so much better to have it than to not!) and various other bits and pieces spread between 3 plastic bags. I had a head torch, spare soft flash and another collapsible cup, this one for hot drinks. On reflection, I think I was going a bit over the top with the cups. My MP3 player, a spare food bar and some waterproof shoe covers were in another bag, and a third had various spare gels, chews and a small pack of cashew nuts. I'd also stuck in a spare peaked cap the evening before, just in case I forgot to pick my favourite one off the radiator in the morning.

The last thing on my pack was a pair of Harrier carbon poles. As I kept trying to remind myself, this was the Green Man, not the Arc of Attrition, but I had a feeling it was going to be muddy, and figured I could always change my mind all the way up until the race start time. If I took them with me, I thoroughly expected to lug them around for 44 of the 45 miles, but I was okay with that.

The final bit of preparation was to stick on my shoes, which still had mud on from whatever fine mess I'd got myself into last time I wore them. Originally bright yellow, I now had a decidedly duller looking pair of Saucony Xodus Ultra's, picked for their reasonable mix of grippiness and comfort on hard trails.

The nice, warm decaffeinated coffee I drank was for one purpose and one purpose only, and it failed to deliver. I said goodbye to Eva and left the house at around 4:45 am, disappointingly not having had to visit the little boy's room.

Half of my stuff went in the boot. I put my race vest in the passenger seat, strapped in with the seatbelt (more to stop the water bottles leaking than because I was worried about its safety). The flask with proper caffeinated Americano went in the cup holder, my phone went on charge, and a 2-litre bottle of water I'd got my son to buy the previous day was tucked in next to my race vest. Android Auto was poked and sworn at for a minute until I had "Ashton Park School, Gatehouse Entrance" set as my destination. At 4:47 am, I drove off the driveway towards Brizzle.

# 3

*Hyperdrive*

## Saturday 2nd March 2024, 04:47

Driving before 5 o'clock in the morning is a pretty nice experience. I had the roads to myself, and I could pootle along at whatever speed I fancied without a BMW up my arse. It was cold outside, and took a while for the windscreen to clear, so much so that on quieter roads I couldn't tell if the window was misted or there was fog outside.

As I headed north past Blandford, I could see white on the verges. It looked like frost, but after a while there seemed to a bit too much of it to be just frozen grass and I started to think there might have been a little snow during the night.

By the time I passed Melbury Abbas and reached Shaftesbury, it was obvious there had been a good flutter of the white stuff. Thankfully, even at this time in the morning, it was confined to the verges, with whatever traffic that had passed since it had fallen having cleared the road.

I kept driving along, quite excited at seeing a bit of snow around – as I said before, on the south coast it's a rare occurrence. I've been told it's something to do with the warm air from the channel, the Purbeck Hills near where I live, and the South Downs off in the other direction, all working together to create a microclimate that is not generally conducive to snow.

I was listening to a new audiobook in the Orphan X series, but only half concentrating as I was both enjoying and slightly wary of the snow on the ground. I decided to switch to music as it didn't require as much concentration. The swigs of coffee I kept drinking were having an effect, as was the music when I stuck on Bring me The Horizon and reminisced about going with my youngest to see them in Bournemouth just over a month before. I was beginning to get in the mood for a race.

It wasn't long before "it had snowed" turned into "it's snowing!", and I found myself driving along a dual carriageway at 20-something miles per hour, a fair distance behind a van but with my windscreen wipers rapidly whisking the flakes off the window to keep my visibility up. I'm not very used to driving in snow, so I stayed slow, not wanting to overtake. I felt in control at a low speed in the tracks of the vehicle in front, but didn't really want to go trying anything exciting.

After a few minutes, the map on the screen in the car showed a turn to the left, and without really thinking, I took it. It didn't take long to realise that Google had decided to take me the most direct route which, instead of sticking to decent main roads, cut through some minor villages on tiny roads in order to shave off half a mile of distance. The snow was heavy now, and I was driving on completely white, quiet roads that hadn't yet been touched by early morning traffic. In short, I was in the shit.

No one else was about, so when I stopped at a small roundabout, I took a couple of photos out the window just so I could capture the experience, otherwise I wasn't sure I'd believe it later in the day. With the wind blowing towards me and the car headlights shining forwards, the photo was quite reminiscent of when the hyperdrive was active in the Millenium Falcon!

I was somewhere near Bath. The sky was dark, but both the road and the air were bright with snow. I was crawling along, at times loving the insane slipperiness of my rear-wheel drive electric car in the snow, and then panicking when I felt that I had absolutely no control over which direction I was going in. I reigned in the entertainment and tried to keep going in a vaguely straight line.

Crossing the brow of a hill, I started descending and wondered why 4 cars on the other side, headlights blazing, were just stopped waiting. As I passed them, I realised that they weren't waiting out of choice – they'd lost any kind of traction on the way up the hill and were waiting to about-turn and descend back down, either for another go or to find a different route. I suddenly realised that, despite the snow being pretty and quite exciting, there was a fairly high chance I wasn't going to get to Bristol today. The satnav said I still had an hour to go, and I didn't think it would be more than 10 minutes before I hit a patch of trouble I couldn't get out of.

Luckily, things worked out in my favour. I did come to a big uphill section, but it had enough tree cover that the road was fairly clear of snow, and I made my way to the top. I soon got to a roundabout back on the main road, and although it was still snowing, the increased traffic made everything much more passable.

The snow lasted until the outskirts of Bristol, but as I got closer to the school it all but disappeared, becoming just a figment of my imagination. I was going to have to check my phone photos to make sure I hadn't just dreamt up the whole thing!

There are too many bus lanes and odd junctions in Bristol, and I made a couple of mistakes in the city. I found myself next to a blue car for a while which didn't seem to know where it was going either – we kept swapping places when hesitating, only to change back again a little later. When I finally reached Ashton Court school, I found myself behind the blue car I'd been jostling with through Bristol.

At the entrance I was directed to the parking area, and I had to sit and wait while the blue car took about 38 attempts to reverse park – it took so long it was becoming ridiculous, but I was pretty sure I was going to bump into the people shortly so didn't want to obviously laugh out loud. I'm pretty crap at reverse parking but they gave a masterclass in fucking it up!

When I was finally ensconced in my parking space, I sat and took a few breaths, relieved and slightly amazed that I had actually made it to the start at all, let alone in plenty of time for the race. It was almost exactly 7 o'clock, and with an hour until the start I decided I had enough time to come back to the car after I'd sorted everything out at registration. Although there was a mandatory kit list, there was no kit check for this race, so I left my pack in the car and walked the few minutes round to the school entrance.

As I wandered along the path, I looked over to the left onto the playing fields, alternating orange and white Ultrarunning Ltd flags forming a corridor to the inflatable orange finish gantry. The weather was dull and grey, but bright flags added an element of excitement to the whole proceedings.

A very cheerful chap directed me into the front entrance, and I stepped inside to a bustling atrium. There were a lot of runners around, and the familiar smell of Deep Heat lingered in the air, mixed in with the loud, nervous chattering of runners. At the desk I gave my name and was rewarded with number 222, and a minute later, after just one attempt, it was pinned neatly to my shorts. I really am starting to get good at pinning numbers on, even if I do say so myself!

I figured it was only going to get busier, so now was probably a good time to use the toilet. I remembered that there were toilets upstairs which were quieter, but it looks like the secret was out as there was a decent sized queue when I got there. When it came to my turn, I was quietly dismayed to find that the lock was missing on the door – bloody school kids wrecking the place! Thankfully, I didn't get interrupted, and was back downstairs a few minutes later, feeling a lot more comfortable.

I walked back to the car, and having spent some time outside of the nicely heated environment of my car and the school, I was becoming acutely aware of just how cold it actually was. According to my phone, the temperate was currently 1°C, but felt like -2°C, which seemed about right according to my rapidly numbing fingers.

Back at the car, I did a quick bit of kit rearranging having now assessed the weather. I took the fingerless gloves out of my bag – they're useful in warm weather to stop the hand straps of my poles rubbing my hands raw, but today, I felt like I'd be wearing proper, warm gloves a fair amount instead. I also took out the backup peaked cap I had in the back as I'd remembered to pick up my favourite one from the radiator earlier, and it was currently perched on top of my head.

I sat in the car, drinking water from the now half-depleted 2 litre bottle. I'd been alternating between the coffee and water on the drive up and was fairly well hydrated now. I stuck some more Bring me The Horizon on, closed my eyes and tried to relax for a few minutes.

I remembered the shoe covers I'd stuffed into the car's armrest and dug out a few pairs to put into the back of my pack. *Why shoe covers?* I hear you ask. Well, one of the race rules stated that outdoor shoes weren't allowed in the checkpoint buildings (or in the school at the end of the race) because of the inevitable mud – without this rule, the cleanup operation would be monumental.

There was no way I was going to take my shoes off (I'd never get them back on again!), so I had the genius idea of buying a load of plastic shoe covers from Amazon. At the cost of carrying an extra 2 grams, I now wouldn't have to remove my shoes, and could enjoy the added bonus of looking like a forensic pathologist at a crime scene. What's not to love?

At just after 7:30, I got out the car and put on the blue Spine jacket from my pack. I dig out my Rab gloves, and stuck a buff around my neck too. I was nice and warm now, and my pack felt quite a bit lighter than it had, which was nice. I put my phone into battery-saver mode, stuck it in a bright green waterproof poo bag and put it in my vest pocket.

The car next to me was open, its owner sorting through his stuff in the boot. On a whim, I offered him some shoe covers – I had about 50 pairs stashed in the car. After I explained why I had them, he decided I wasn't completely insane, accepted a couple, and thanked me. With that, I headed back to the hall, just as a gentle rain began to fall.

Because of the rain, we all crammed into the building for the race briefing, which was presented by a lady from half way up the staircase. She told us that despite there not being much snow around this area, we would start seeing it on the route after checkpoint 2. I was quite excited by this – it's not every day you get real snow in an ultra! She told us to be careful on the road crossings, of which there were quite a few.

Some chap called Ian had run around the whole route in barefoot shoes within the last week, and had confirmed that, although there was plenty of mud, the whole of the route had been accessible, with no trees down or flooded areas. That was good to know.

The final point made was that we weren't to go inside any of the checkpoint buildings unless shoes were off. I stood smugly, with my stash of shoe covers secreted inside my pack.

We all bustled from the warmth of the building to the cold, wetter outside area. It wasn't raining much, but it was enough to warrant having my coat hood up, and I could feel the cold seeping through to my hands despite having my gloves on. Still, once we got going, I was pretty sure I'd be too hot quite quickly.

I spotted Giacomo Squintani in the crowd, and our eyes met. He came over and we had a bit of a chat about the day. I first met Gia doing this very race back in 2015, when I overtook him right at the end of the race. We've stayed in touch ever since and ran several of the same races at the same time – generally not together though, as he's a better runner than I am. He's also almost 12 years into a run streak too – running every single day for over 4,000 days is mind-blowing!

There was some excited activity beside us, and everyone started bunching up towards the start line. Once we were all nicely packed together, a countdown started somewhere, and we all joined in from 10.

When it reached zero, 196 runners headed off on what was sure to be a muddy and exciting 45-mile circumnavigation of Bristol.

# 4

*A fair bit of concentration*

## Saturday 2nd March 2024, 08:00

| Start | |
|---|---|
| Time | 8:00 am |
| Competitors Starting | 196 |

When the best part of 200 people charge off across a wet grassy playing field in luggy trail shoes, the ground quickly becomes a bit of a quagmire as those of us towards the back end of the pack soon found out.

I started slowly, thinking that this was a long race so there's plenty of time to adjust, but very soon I was having a nagging feeling that I should be going faster. I mostly do long ultramarathons – 100 or more miles – so 45 miles is a quick jog, right? No need to hold back, I might as well push on. I went wide of the main group, and ran along, overtaking great swathes of people and feeling rather pleased with myself. When I look back, it amazes me how much of an idiot I can be sometimes!

A wide gate was open in the fence line of the school and there was plenty of room for us all to get through without any problems, then head up a nice tarmac road into the Ashton Court estate. A left turn took us onto a flinty path continuing upwards, the spiky rocks underfoot requiring a bit of concentration to make sure there were no trips.

My breathing was a bit heavier than I would have expected or liked, but I hadn't felt quite right for most of the last 3 months. Running was just a little more of an effort than it should have been, and I hadn't been enjoying many runs while trying to push out the weekly mileage. But here, in a race, there's that element of adventure and fun, of competition and camaraderie, and a bit of heavier breathing at the start was something that could be ignore. At least that's what I hoped.

We came to a gate. A crowd of runners hitting a narrow kissing gate en masse is always going to cause a bit of a traffic jam, and I found myself at the back of a queue of about 10 people, slowly making their way one-by-one through the gate. As I waited, someone went past and climbed over the closed bar-gate adjacent to the footpath, and seconds later it was like being at the Grand National with loads of people bounding and leaping over the gate!

I watched on enviously as people made their way much faster over the gate, but like a British person in a supermarket queue, I stood my ground, convinced that changing lanes was a bad idea. It wasn't long before I got through the gate, by which time almost everyone I'd passed with my burst of effort earlier had gone past me again.

After the gate, the path got flintier, and the dips and bumps formed the perfect surface for puddles to form. Most of the people ahead were doing their best to avoid the water, switching left and right, tiptoeing around the dips. I'd once been told by a race director that not only will that wear you out more, you're also more likely to injure yourself by trying to avoid every puddle. If it's a muddy run, embrace it! So, I did, heading straight through all but the deepest pools, trying my very best not to splash anyone near me.

My breathing wasn't settling, which was starting to annoy me. My legs felt okay, I didn't feel like I was going too fast, and yet I sounded like someone at the end of a parkrun PB attempt. I tried to keep ignoring it, telling myself that it was very early in the race. I noticed there wasn't a lot of chatter going on around me, which suggested that everyone was working a bit here. There was nothing unusual going on with me, I told myself, I just needed to relax and settle in to the race.

The terrain required a fair bit of concentration as we went up the path under trees. The rocks, dips, puddles and now tree roots kept me on my toes (literally) until I reached a gap in a stone wall that led onto a road crossing. At the briefing, I thought we had been told that this crossing would be marshalled, but there was no one here. Maybe I was in a group that was so far ahead that I'd arrived before the marshal? Or, far more likely, I'd just misheard the details.

The route took us through part of Long Ashton Golf Club, with the path taking the high ground around the edge of the course. The wet grass and the slope down to the greens made running awkward, with my feet constantly sliding sideways on the hill. Fortunately, it wasn't long before we left the golf course and hit a section of the course I hadn't been looking forward to.

The muddy path started descending fairly steeply and turned from tree roots on dirty ground to a deep rut of yellow-orange clay which, from previous experience, I knew was as slippery as hell. I made my way slowly along the path, noticing only a couple of people ahead and wondering if I'd somehow moved forward again – in previous races, this section had been much busier.

The trees grew up all around, and their roots poked out into and under the clay ahead forming an uneven path of lumps, bumps and the occasional hole. After not many steps at all, the soles of my shoes were caked with a layer of clay which totally removed any grip, and I tentatively made my way along, holding on to tree branches where possible to arrest any slips.

I was aware of someone very close behind me and, not wanting to hold them up, I pulled in to the side.

"I'm taking it really slowly down here; I remember what this bit is like!" I explained. "You go on ahead."

The guy shot past, and as I resumed my slow, careful descent, I watched as he slipped and almost tripped 3 times before we each reached the end of the clay bit.

A small, dispersed group of us descended a steep but solid path and I recognised this as the point where I passed Gia at the end of the race back in 2015.

It's worth clarifying something here – in my 5 times of starting the Green Man Ultra since 2014, there have been 3 different start (and end) locations. The first time was at the Brook Redwood Hotel, which was about 1 kilometre to the west of where I was now. In 2015, the Race HQ was at Long Ashton Community Centre, which I was just about to pass as I ran down the hill and hence was right near the end of the race. And in 2017, 2022 and this year, it's all kicked off from Ashton Park School.

Although my memory was of blasting down this hill, almost sprinting to the finish just metres away, there was no chance

I'd be doing that today as the stony ground was wet with rain and had the potential to be very slippery. The rain was still falling but had subsided to a level where it wasn't worth having my hood up. With my coat, long sleeved top and base layer on, I was comfortably warm now after just over 2 miles of running, and having spent a while descending, my breathing felt much better. I was beginning to enjoy myself!

After the first couple of miles of paths and woods we were now heading along the roads of a housing estate. The route took us more-or-less south, with a few turns at road junctions to keep us going in that direction. There were some groups of people hanging around on corners, obviously crew or support for runners, but they were mostly silent or chatting amongst themselves, so there wasn't much of an atmosphere – no clapping, cheering or general encouragement, which was a bit unusual for a race. I suppose it wasn't the sort of weather that was easy to enjoy being out in.

It was an easy part of the course. Although I was running on my own, there were single runners and the odd pair or group of 3 making their way ahead, which meant I didn't need to look at my watch – just follow the line. Everyone was running about the same speed, so we just stayed spread out in our positions and headed along the roads.

At the bottom of the housing estate was a bridge over the railway line between Nailsea & Backwell and Parson Street stations. The bridge was like a portal to a new dimension – no more solid tarmac streets, instead replaced with a sea of gloopy mud that resembled chocolate mousse so thick it completely enveloped my feet.

After squelching through the mud-soup, we hit wet, manky and still muddy grass which descended some wooden steps into woods. I found myself at the front of a group with no one to follow, so I kept trying to follow the track on my watch, but the sketchy steps, tree routes and generally uneven ground required concentration, making it very difficult to figure out the twists and turns on the little screen. At the bottom of the hill, tall concrete stilts carried the main A370 above our heads, and my gut feeling was to head under the road, a sparkle of a memory somewhere at the back of my head. The guy behind me agreed, and we both continued along the path. After a minute of the map jumping about on the screen, my watch settled down and confirmed we'd gone the right way.

The woodland trail kept on going for a while. The route wasn't always particularly obvious, but through a combination of my watch track and the occasional Community Forest Path marker on a post, stile or bridge, I kept to the right track. We passed along the edge of Woodspring golf course, and next to the three massive Barrow Gurney Reservoirs, capable of supplying a massive 140 million litres of drinking water a day. Then, as suddenly as it had started, the muddy path ended as I passed between two houses and found myself on the edge of the A38.

Despite still not being heavy, the rain steadfastly refused to completely stop, and the surface water led to blasts of noise as the traffic went past on the busy road. I kept looking behind as I ran along, and on spotting a gap in the traffic I crossed to the other side of the road. I was initially pleased that it had been relatively easy to cross the road, but when a big Range Rover went past me and sent the contents of a massive puddle all over me, I wasn't quite so sure that I'd made the right decision to cross early! Before I turned off the short stretch of road, I was shivering with the cold from my unexpected shower.

Now began the largest climb on the whole course, about 450 feet up to the top of Dundry Hill. It started with more mud soup as the line of runners passed a farmhouse, went through a gate and ended up on a narrow path that started to ascend. I was conscious of people behind me and didn't want to hold anyone up and so, despite not wanting to, I picked up pace to a run, making use of the temporarily solid ground.

The path opened out onto more soft, muddy grass, and the climb stood before us. Considering the state of the ground as I climbed, it seemed like now would be a very good time to use my poles, so they came out the quiver and were soon providing me with some extra help as I made my way upwards. It turns out they were quite an asset, as while others were slipping and sliding on the grass having trouble getting any sort of traction, I just kept going, overtaking quite a few people.

I crossed a stile onto a tarmac road, but within 30 seconds I had turned back off onto a muddy path, so kept the poles out as they were still helping.

Near the top of Dundry Hill almost 700 feet above sea level is the largest of 7 towers, almost 200ft tall and covered with antennae. It's a nice thing to pass in the race, as it means not only is there no more climbing for a while, but at no point for the rest of the race do you go much more than half as high as this hill again.

I checked the time on my watch and was a bit disappointed. This was the first of the few timing points I'd put on my chart, and my optimistic target had me here at 8:58 am. My watch showed just before 9:01 am. Less than 3 minutes late, but late nonetheless. With the way my breathing had been, the occasional bursts of speed I'd put in, and the points where I'd been running when I didn't really want to be, I had hoped that I would be a few minutes *ahead* of the target time. Where I'd been looking forward to easing back, safe in the knowledge I was going a little faster than I needed, I was now going to have work even harder.

At least it was easier terrain now, with a solid track that ran between the antenna tower and the village ahead. The track was rutted and uneven, lots of big puddles dotted about to keep my feet nice and wet. I did, however, pass the first lot of people waiting by the side of the path that were clapping and cheering us on, and it was nice to have some encouragement.

My right shoe felt a bit loose. I made a mental note to tighten it at checkpoint 1. I couldn't remember exactly how far away the checkpoint was, but I figured it couldn't be all that far. A couple of button presses on my watch would have shown me, but at that point, I wasn't really all that interested in the details.

I hadn't been drinking much so far, probably because I was nicely hydrated after glugging all that water on the drive to Bristol earlier, but after the hill climb I was quite warm and, for the first time, a little thirsty. I leant down and took a big glug from the bottle in my vest, managing to accidentally pull off the rubber top from the bottle. I stopped immediately so as not to squeeze the now open bottle which sat benignly in my vest pocket, and I carefully squeezed the top back onto the bottle without much in the way of spillage. That could have been a real disaster – losing a load of water and getting myself soaking in the process!

I was carrying my poles as I went through the village, just contemplating collapsing them and putting them back in the quiver, when I met a couple of guys coming towards me.

"Turn around, this is the wrong way," one said, and a quick look on my watch showed that the correct route was a lefthand fork just back from where I was.

It wasn't long before the road turned to a track and we were back in that irritating thick mud again; I was glad I hadn't put my poles away and could use them for a bit of stability. After a short stretch with a couple of stiles and some 90-degree turns, we were back out on a lane that crossed over a busier looking road at the top of a hill. The junction looked strangely familiar, and I figured I must have driven past it on route to the start that morning. I could hear the sound of a struggling engine coming up the hill but looking both ways didn't reveal anything about to immediately flatten me, so I took up a little jog and crossed the road onto East Dundry Lane.

This was a good section of road, nice and solid, not busy, and with a very gentle downhill slope. There were a few little groups of runners making their way along, and there were the first signs of snow on the verges of the road. Not too much of the white stuff here, but the occasional glimpse of a view down the hill showed significant blankets here and there in the direction we were heading. Exciting stuff!

As gentle, comfortable and enjoyable as the road was, all good things must come to an end and as the line of people ahead veered to the right and disappeared through the hedge, I followed into a grassy field which continued the downward sloping trend. Again, the poles were useful for traction, and the longer grass did a fine job of absolutely soaking my shoes, socks and feet in icy cold water.

Towards the far end of the field, we encountered a fine example of *Cursus Clickus*, otherwise known as the Race Photographer. Crouching down, he snapped a few shots of people approaching, shouting encouragement as they passed.

"That's a brilliant idea!" he shouted, when it came to my turn. "Those poles, I bet they really help." From the sounds of it, I was the first person to pass by with poles.

"I wasn't sure whether to even bother, but I'm really glad I did. They've been really handy so far," I shouted back as we passed each other.

Somewhere around here, I found myself running at the same sort of pace as Melissa Venables, and we had a lovely chat while running along, watching out for the various turns onto roads and then paths again. We passed through a farm, across more fields and onto some twisting lanes. After a longer stretch on wet grass, we passed through the village of Norton Hawkfield, where we both took the wrong route as we were busy nattering. It wasn't much of an error, but as usual, it added a chunk of unnecessary hill which we then had to return back down to take the entrance of what looked like another farm which we'd missed on the way up.

Half a mile later, we'd bounced off the corner of a field (metaphorically, not literally), passed under a few trees and then come out on a road where something of a crowd had gathered. We had reached Norton Malreward Village Hall, the home of Checkpoint 1.

# 5

*Disappeared downwards*

## Saturday 2nd March 2024, 09:38

| CP1: Norton Malreward | |
|---|---|
| Distance | 9.1 miles |
| Time | 9:38 am (1h 38m) |
| Target Time | 9:33 am (-5 mins) |
| Elevation | 1,268ft/386m |
| Time at Checkpoint | 4 minutes |
| Competitors Remaining | 194 |

I checked my watch and saw I was 5 minutes behind my target time for the checkpoint, but I was just about 5 minutes *ahead* of my 2017 time. That was the year I got my PB for this race, so overall I was actually quite positive, which was a change from how I'd felt back at Dundry. All I had to do now was not waste a load of time.

Over the last half mile or so before the checkpoint, I'd been thinking about what I needed to do: drink, food, and take my long-sleeved top off as I was now getting a bit warm. That loose shoe I'd meant to adjust had somehow managed to tighten itself again, so I'd forgotten about it.

I'd deliberately only been drinking from one water bottle, and with the weather being so cold, I hadn't finished it. That made refilling nice and easy and, as usual, the floppy depleted soft flask was already in my hand as I ran up to the checkpoint desk. I took off my pack, tore open a Tailwind sachet and poured half into the bottle, tucking the other half back in my vest and hoping it wouldn't explode in a puff of stickiness as I ran along. I handed my open bottle to a lady who was waiting to fill bottles and got on with a quick change.

My jacket came off, as did the black top. It was absolutely soaking – I'd probably been a bit warmer than I thought, so it was good to be undoing some of the layers now. It was still only 3 or 4 degrees and hadn't quite managed to stop raining, so I put my coat back on and it felt a lot cooler and fresher with just the t-shirt underneath.

My bottle went back in my vest as I munched my way through a couple of pieces of ginger cake, and then I was pretty much done. I had a quick think to make sure I hadn't forgotten anything, picked up my poles, thanked everyone and headed off. My checkpoint stop had taken 4 minutes.

When I ran this race all the way back in 2014, Norton Malreward had been my first ever ultramarathon checkpoint, and I had a lovely chat with everyone and took over 20 minutes to do whatever the hell I did. When I stepped out the building (the checkpoint was inside back then), I had no idea which direction to go in, had to ask for help, and was told to look out for a hidden turn off the road I was directed up.

With this being the 5th time I've run the race, I knew exactly where I was going, and guided a couple of other people through the tree-covered gap in the hedge into yet another field.

It might be the fifth time, but until reviewing maps after the event, I had no idea that I was just about to cross over Norton Malreward Airstrip, a 580 metre long and 24 metre wide grass strip on a lovely flat field. I'll be keeping my eye out next time I cross to try and spot it and hopefully no one will get flattened by an unexpected landing light aircraft!

I caught up with and started running with a chap who's name I just can't remember, which is annoying, as he had quite a story. He was raising £12,000 for a local hospice, which had been the cost of looking after his grandad for the last 6 months of his life. Since starting training a year ago, he'd lost 40kg and built up to this race, the 45-mile Green Man Ultra, with the aim of completing Ironman Texas next year. He was chirpy, chatty and truly inspirational, and I'm really annoyed that I can't figure out his name!

Over the course of a mile from the airstrip, we lost most of the remaining height gained by that climb up to Dundry, and found ourselves in a very, very soggy field alongside the River Chew. The river looked to me like it had overflowed its banks recently and then receded a little, with big patches of water dotted around the fields. The chap I was running with confirmed that it had been much higher and had gone down quite a bit which I was very glad about – the going would be wet enough even in its current state! He also mentioned that there were otters in this part of the river, so we kept a bit of an eye out, although didn't end up seeing any.

There were plenty of flooded spots on the path, big stretches of water that there was no way of avoiding. The mud turned the puddles an opaque brown-orange so there was no way to see what was under your feet, and I was lifting my feet high and being tentative with my steps so as not to trip.

It came as a bit of a surprise when I put my foot forward and it disappeared downwards into a big hole that I had no idea was there. I almost toppled over, dropping down and instinctively putting my hands out which went all the way up to my elbows in the water before finding solid ground. I gasped from the sudden cold as my knee bent forward, and my shin managed to catch one of my poles hard, which had me yelling out in pain. This was far from ideal!

I got myself up out the water, and limped along a little way so I could assess the damage. My gloves were dripping wet, the inside of my coat sleeves soaked. My legs were dripping, my shin hurt a lot, and my pole had a slight kink along its line. I popped the button to check it still closed and found that two of the 3 sections were now jammed together, and despite a few attempts at pulling and bending, I could not get them to separate. On the plus side, it still worked as a pole when pushed back together, so at least it was stay useful in that respect.

I rubbed my shin and felt quite a significant bump. It stung, but I knew there was no real damage and I was just going to have to ignore it for now – I was pretty sure I would forget about it within a mile or two.

Well, that was exciting! There was an issue, however, aside from my shin and busted pole. Having got myself completely soaked and then stopped for a time, I now felt very cold, and was starting to shiver. I needed to get moving again, so started running along, sploshing towards the edges of the puddles and trying to avoid any more hidden holes.

Just around the corner, we reached part of the course I really like. I'm a big fan of railways and Victorian engineering and, at 303 metres long and 29 metres high, the Pensford Viaduct is a fine example of both of these.

It was built in 1874 for the Bristol and North Somerset Railway to cross the River Chew and was used for passenger trains through to 1959. In 1968, a deluge flooded 88 properties in the village, washed away a road bridge over the A37 and caused enough damage to the viaduct that it would never be opened again. The rain that day was so heavy that it added 2 *billion* litres of water to the Chew Valley Lake, causing serious concern that the dam would breach. Luckily, it didn't.

All 6 million bricks of the viaduct went on sale in 1984 for the princely sum of one English pound. A veritable bargain, one might think, but as the maintenance would then become the responsibility of the owner it was actually a poison chalice, and no one took up the offer. Ownership transferred to the company responsible for British Rail bits and pieces after privatisation, and since 2013, it's been the responsibility of the Highways Agency.

Despite the niggling pain in my shin and the shivering from coldness, I marvelled at the arches and stopped a moment to look up as I ran on the road under the bridge. As I came out from under the bridge, I noticed that, for the first time in the race, it had actually stopped raining.

A small, dispersed group of us ran on into Pensford village, crossed the A37 (presumably on a bridge built after 1968) and followed the road around to the gentle climb of Publow Lane. After a few more minutes of road, we took a pathway to the right, through a gate, and back into the familiar muddy fields.

A pretty much straight line across a field took us to Publow where we ran over Publow Bridge and around the edge of the Church of All Saints before properly embracing the banks of the Chew again. The rain might have stopped, but the temperature seemed to have dropped, and we had a new friend added to the mix. The ground was muddy with patchy grass, all now topped off with a layer of snow.

The snowfall hadn't been major, but it was enough to cover the fields, leaving me with a line of ice-cold slush to run through. The net result was continuously wet feet that were now beginning to freeze. I couldn't feel my toes, and the numbness was starting to work its way along my feet, removing any real sensation of what I was landing on. Luckily, it was pretty stable and easy terrain so I didn't fall over or twist an ankle, but I wasn't enjoying the pain that was beginning to burn from the ice cold at the front of my feet.

My combination of running and walking slowed to mostly walking, and a few people went past me. The odd one stopped for a bit of a chat, but the pain in my toes was beginning to become all encompassing so I wasn't much company.

It wasn't all snow – there were still plenty of big unavoidable puddles, and strangely the water in those actually felt warm for a moment on my feet, so I didn't mind splashing through. It wasn't a clever strategy, though, as they got even colder afterwards. The ground was soft, muddy and energy sapping, and at no point would I say it was remotely easy going.

Judging by the continuous flow of people passing me, I was slowing down quite significantly. The lack of any sensation other than a thumping pain in my feet was mostly to blame, and I didn't have any real choice other than to keep slow and steady. At this point, I was incredibly grateful for having had the foresight to pack my poles, although my hands were now starting to numb from being wrapped in cold, wet gloves. Each time I came to a stile, if there was anyone remotely close behind, I would let them go first as I was taking ages to climb over each one.

A little over 3 miles of mostly ice cold, wet fields since skirting around the church at Publow, I found myself on solid ground. I went through the courtyard area of Albert Mill, a Grade II listed watermill and the first building we came to on the southern edge of Keynsham – I knew there were no more muddy fields until after the checkpoint now, which made me very happy.

I wasn't so much in a group as a spaced-out train now, with a few people running ahead, and a few behind. I picked up to a run even though I still couldn't really feel my feet, but the flat tarmac path was easy to move over. The route took us through the park, and I passed the Keynsham Coffee Co based out of one of those shiny metal trailers, the guy inside looking very animated and cheerful (probably because of how much he's making!). I would have stopped and grabbed a cup of decent coffee if it wasn't for the length of the queue extending out of the hatch.

I carried on along the path adjacent to the river, under a couple of road bridges, then followed the path around to the right. I couldn't quite make out where I was supposed to go, and it seemed I wasn't the only one as a guy in front had just stopped to take a proper look at his watch map. I caught up with him, and we both decided that it looked like we were supposed to go up the grassy hill ahead to the road, although the top of the hill just looked like a continuous fence of metal railings with no way to get through. The hill didn't look very appealing either as it was muddy and quite steep, but it wasn't far so we both decided to give it a go.

At the top was a gate which has been hidden from view by a bush, so with some relief we went through onto the pavement. We went under the railway line and continued in a straight line towards the bridge that would take us over the river and to the checkpoint. The guy I was running with explained that his partner was going to meet him just ahead, so he went in a different direction as I turned right onto the road over the River Avon.

After crossing the river, from my higher vantage point on the bridge I could see the checkpoint off to my right and down below. I continued along the remainder of the road to the turn off a little way ahead. I passed through a little tunnel of people clapping as I descended the steps, then turned back on myself and crossed over a much older bridge which had played a part in the English Civil War as the Roundheads saved the town. Just ahead was the car park of the Lock Keeper, an early 18th pub and site of the Green Man Ultra checkpoint 2.

# 6

*Field. Stile. Field. Stile. Field. Stile.*

## Saturday 2nd March 2024, 11:03

| CP2: Keynsham ||
|---|---|
| Distance (from previous) | 16.4 (7.3) miles |
| Time (from previous) | 11:03 am (1h 25m) |
| Target Time | 10:45 am (-18 mins) |
| Elevation (from previous) | 1,889ft/576m (621ft/189m) |
| Time at Checkpoint | 2 minutes |
| Competitors Remaining | 189 |

Two minutes. That's how long I spent at checkpoint 2. I had my bottle in hand again as I reached the table that was set up with water and snacks and managed to reach around to pull out the half-used stick of Tailwind without having to take my pack off.

A sweet lady with a foreign accent from somewhere that I couldn't place filled up my water bottle and chatted with me, bringing a really positive feeling to the whole encounter. I stuffed in another slice of ginger cake, squeezed the now full bottle back into my vest, grabbed another piece of cake and got going. I didn't realise it at the time, but the 30-mile race had set off under the bridge I'd crossed at 11 am, just a couple of minutes before I arrived.

From the pub car park, the route takes you momentarily back up the way I came but then veers off to the left to head under the big bridge I'd crossed over. On the other side, the path which was just a brown strip of mud cut along the edge of yet another grassy field with Keynsham Lock to the left. Construction on the lock started 300 years ago to the year, all the way back in 1724, and took 3 years to complete – so boats have been passing by this strip of land for three centuries. Quite amazing, when you stop to think about it!

What was less amazing was the mud. There were a few stiles and gates along this stretch of path, and each one was surrounded by a huge, unavoidable puddle of thick brown mud. Given the current state of my feet – cold, wet and muddy – it didn't really make a huge difference, but every time I had to negotiate one, I had to take slow, timid steps through the squelch to make sure I didn't end up on my arse.

On the plus side, I was definitely a bit warmer. My feet were still cold but not thumping painfully with every step. My hands were still numb, but that wasn't unusual as I've suffered from Raynaud's for the last 20 years or so and was used to having painful stumps on the end of my arms when it got cold. It did occur to me that having just a single layer – my short-sleeved compression top – on underneath my coat probably wasn't a great idea, but if I kept moving, I'd stay just about warm enough. And besides, I just didn't have the dexterity in my hands to fiddle around with pack straps and zips to get my long-sleeved top out, which was something that – with hindsight – I should never, ever have let happen.

There wasn't much in the way of socialising going on here. There were one or two runners ahead of me, and one or two behind, but we were all just running or walking along in our own bubble of concentration. I was overtaken when I came to a couple of particularly narrow stiles. The planks were sodden and slippery, and my hands were of little use, so I was again very slow at making my way over the top.

A mile on from the checkpoint was the village of Willsbridge, where I followed a short stretch of the A341 then crossed over to take a woodland path, the entrance gap in the stone wall familiar from previous Green Man runs. The path led uphill next to Siston Brook, under thick tree cover, over stone steps with occasional moss-covered walls to the sides. There were a few couples and families out for a walk despite the weather, and I carefully made my way around them so as not to be too irritating.

The path opened out to Willsbridge Mill, an early 18th century watermill originally used for milling corn to produce flour, but later changed to linseed, used in the production of paints and varnishes. Operation ceased in the mid-20th century, and the mill is now a community and educational resource with a nice-looking coffee shop, which I think was the big draw for most of the non-runners out and about today. To the right of the mill, on a well maintained if a little muddy gravel path, stood the Dramway.

Opened in 1832, the Dramway was a tram line that ran from Coalpit Heath through Warmley, Willsbridge (where I was now), and onwards to the River Avon. Horse-drawn wagons known as 'drams' ran on iron rails and were used to transport coal from the mines to barges on the river for onward transportation. With the advent of steam railways, the Dramway fell out of use in the mid-18th century, and most of its length is now a shared walking and cycling trail.

I was starting to feel a bit tired now, having been going for over 3 hours and covering just under 18 miles. Luckily, the ground ahead was solid and decent to run along, the puddles mostly easily avoidable, and after less than half a mile I was back out on a street among houses. Guided by my watch, a couple of turns and an alleyway later, I was on the Bristol & Bath Railway footpath next to the 3 miles of very real train tracks that carried the heritage Avon Valley Railway.

The nice thing about railways – from a runner's perspective at least – is that trains can't go up or down very steep hills, so the adjacent path was essentially flat. The down side is that, on a flat path, there's no excuse not to run and so, reluctantly, off I went along the mile or so of tarmac at a slow but consistent plod.

I quickly became fed up with holding my poles, so I collapsed them down. One folded completely, but the other one I'd bent earlier would only fold at one section. With no other choice, I reached behind me and stashed them away in the quiver, one pole poking high above my head like some sort of flag. It wobbled around a bit, but I soon forgot about it and just got on with running along and avoiding the puddles.

One year when I was running along this section, a steam train passed by on the tracks, which was a lovely experience. All the noise of the engine and the clickity-clack of the carriages completely absorbing my attention for a good few minutes. But today, the tracks were silent, and all I had to concentrate on was the back of the runners ahead who, amazingly, I seemed to be very slowly gaining on.

I ran under a few bridges, exchanging greetings with people out for a gentle morning run under gloomy skies, going in the opposite direction to me. I kept looking at my watch, which showed a right turn ahead signalling the end of this path. I couldn't remember exactly what happened at the turn, but my memory was of there being a bridge over the railway. I guess I'd find out in 0.75 miles.

The three-quarters of a mile took a little over 5 minutes of running, at which point the path came to a pedestrian crossing which crossed a busy looking road. I had been completely wrong about the bridge over the railway, and it was only as I thought about it now that I realised the railway track had come to an end quite a way back along the path.

I had to cross the road, but it was busy and I wasn't going to wait for the lights to change on the crossing, so I took the right turn on the pavement and kept an eye on the traffic. The area didn't feel at all familiar, but I was clearly following the route indicated on my watch.

I think I must have hit a rare moment of heavy traffic on the road, as soon it was pretty much empty and I crossed over easily, taking a left into a very industrial looking road. There were big buildings to each side, iron fences and lots of cars parked on one side of the road.

"Are you heading to Ashton?" asked a guy who was walking towards me with his dog.

"Yeah, that's right." I figured he was going to give me the usual bit of encouragement or incredulity, but instead he gave me directions.

"You need to go up there," he said, pointing at a pathway hidden behind the trees that I was just about to run past as it was easy to miss. I thanked him and got off the road back onto the Dramway. On looking at maps after the race, I can see the

Dramway actually starts on the previous road so, instead of turning onto this industrial estate road, if I'd continued another 10 metres or so along, I could have joined there. Something to remember for next time, not that it would really make any difference.

The path quickly turned to mud again, but it wasn't long before I was back on a short stretch of road that took me past a bunch of bright red houses. Another brown, muddy trail appeared under trees between two houses, and my watch pushed me in that direction.

The Texas Ironman guy that I had run with a few hours before had mentioned that most of the Dramway had been underwater a few weeks before. It wasn't now, but there was a *lot* of mud along this stretch, with several big stretches of water that covered the path and were unavoidable. There were plenty of tree branches across the path too, which wouldn't have been a problem ducking under if it hadn't been for my broken pole sticking out the top of my bag which kept catching and yanking me back. I was having to squat down really low to get under some of the obstructions – a good workout for the legs, but not great for progress on tired legs a few hours into a race.

After half a mile of sploshing and ducking, I arrived in Warmley alongside an inviting 8-foot-tall spiky metal fence. Another quick jaunt along a road and I was back onto the familiar path under trees and through mud. There were a few runners around here, quite a bit of swearing about the state of the ground, and generally slow progress northwards. After half a mile of muddy forest tracks, a group of us crossed a road and took a track up between two lovely looking houses which soon ended at a metal gate, the ubiquitous muddy grassy path on the other side.

Field. Stile. Field. Stile. Field. Stile.

The snow came back.

My feet froze.

My hands went numb.

The stiles were slippery, and I let a few people pass, but the spacing was meaning I was standing around for too long, so I also ended up with a group of people bunching up behind me with my pathetically slow traversal of the fences.

I tried to run, but it's difficult when you can't feel your feet.

Field. Stile. Field. Stile.

I remembered listening to Noel Gallagher's High Flying Birds album *Chasing Yesterday* running across this field. The album was new at the time, so it must have been 2015. It wasn't cold back then. My feet didn't feel like they'd been hit with a hammer. In fact, I seem to remember it being a bit on the warm side, quite unlike now. Again, I thought about wanting more layers on, but there was no way my hands would be able to do anything useful like that, so I just had to make do with what I had on. *As soon as I warm up a bit*, I told myself, *I'll get it sorted*. All I had to do was remember at the right time.

The final field gave way to the final stile which I didn't need to rush over as the people behind were a bit of a way back. I took my time, got onto the edge of the B4465 and took advantage of a handy lack of traffic to cross to the other side.

There was a road directly ahead which wasn't the one to take – my watch said I should continue a little way further up the road to the right. As I was on more solid ground, I started very slowly running, passing the driveway to a house and onwards towards the bus stop ahead, behind which, for some reason, I presumed the path would start.

A fortuitous glance at my watch showed that I'd actually *passed* the turn I needed to take, and I looked behind to see the people who had been behind me heading up that house driveway that I'd just passed. I ran back down and saw that in the corner just ahead was a gate that led back onto the Community Forest Path.

The path continued under a bit more tree cover, which meant no snow and gave my feet a chance to start warming up. There was a short stretch of road, then we rejoined the Dramway track and passed the back of the now closed Shortwood Landfill site. Random fact: the license for the landfill site allowed them to take 200,000 tonnes of waste each year for 10 years, a total of 2 million cubic metres of rubbish!

We soon came to a scarred area of land with a prominent grey and red chimney clearly visible. Information signs just off the path told me that this was Brandy Bottom Colliery. For 99 years from 1837 through to 1936, this steam-powered colliery dragged coal from the ground, dumping it into drams for the horses to carry away to the river on the very Dramway that I was running along.

Navigation was easy here – I just had to keep the people ahead in sight. I ran when I could, and it seemed I was a little faster than those around me but couldn't keep it up for long. I'd run for a bit, catch up with a group, then slow back down to a walk – I didn't want to overtake only to have to then come to an awkward stop just in front of people. On average, we seemed to be moving around the same sort of pace.

On the far side of the field, a raised embankment carried 6 lanes of the M4 motorway, and ahead of us was a tunnel which took the Community Forest Path under the road. A single road cone stood smack bang in the wide tunnel entrance, foretelling of a great flood ahead! It wasn't ideal, but without taking a bloody great diversion, this was the way we had to go, and it's not like my feet hadn't been wet so far today. I sploshed in, wondering just how deep it would get.

Not all that deep, I found. It was above my shoes, but not for long, and by half way through the tunnel, the concrete ground was dry again. Which is more than could be said for the field on the far side.

I ran – or rather squelched – my way along, chatting to an Irish bloke with an impressive beard. He mentioned he'd done an ultra across Scotland where he lived, which I'm guessing was the GB Ultra Race Across Scotland. A friend of mine – Bea Griffiths – has run it, and at 215 miles with 100 hours to complete it, sounds like a walk in the park compared to the Green Man! (Just to be clear, I'm being *very* sarcastic here!).

Being in far better condition than I was, the bearded Irish chap was soon a figure in the distance as I plodded my way through the thick, sinking grasses. My breathing was unusually heavy again, as it had been each and every time I exerted myself. I was getting used to it, and quite frankly a bit surprised that I could be breathing this hard for so much of the race and still keep going.

Like a lot of places in the race, this field had memories. In 2017, I'd run the race with my friend Rob. He likes to swear, as I do but, being Irish, he was a bit better at it than me. Nothing was sacred – trees, sheep, fences, the motorway, houses – everything we passed was shouted at and called a variety of words beginning with F, C, W, T and many other letters of the alphabet! It was all done with smiles and laughter, and I have no real idea *why* we did it – I think it was just one of those moments in an ultra where it felt like the right thing to do.

A slightly less amusing memory was from 2015, when I ran out of water here. As I've already mentioned, it was much, much warmer than today, bordering on what could be legitimately described as hot, and with just under 5 miles to the next checkpoint, I had a pretty miserable time. Although I probably didn't really *need* the water, having none meant it became a focus, then an all-encompassing obsession, and I was ridiculously happy when I finally got to the checkpoint and gulped down a few cups.

Today, however, I was on my own. There was no one to swear at inanimate objects with, and I had plenty of water. I was absolutely fucking freezing; I couldn't feel my hands and my feet were agony. I wanted to dig into my bag, delve into the drybag that I brought along for emergencies, and get out the lightweight fleece I had packed with no intention whatsoever of needing, but there was absolutely no point in stopping. My stupid bloody hands were as useful as stumps.

I learnt a very big lesson today: sort out your clothes BEFORE you get too cold, as when your hands become useless, your options are severely limited. There was a great danger that today, this mistake was going to cost me my race.

# 7

*Then all hell broke loose*

## Saturday 2nd March 2024, 12:48

The wet, muddy fields eventually succumbed to the tarmac strip of Westerley Road, and I followed the line on my watch directly across the road into a side road called Boxhedge Farm Lane. A little white VW had just driven through a significant flood across the road and had luckily managed to survive all the way to the junction. I sploshed through yet another ankle-deep flood without giving it much thought. It wasn't like I was going to get any colder or wetter.

The road turned back onto a track that ran along the edge of 3 more fields, then out onto another road. A bit of junction negotiation guided in part by my watch and partly from a vague familiarity of the area, and at just before 1 o'clock I turned onto a half mile long uphill stretch of Henfield Road.

There were lots of puddles on the edges of the road, and it had started raining again, heavier than in the morning to the point where I had pulled my hood up and could feel the rain dripping off the bottom of my coat. There were no pavements on this part of the road, and avoiding the puddles meant moving out into the road where possible, but there was enough occasional traffic to mean that I had to sometimes either stop or splosh through a puddle. I chose the latter – it was easier than stopping and starting back up again.

A pavement appeared, which made things a bit easier. I was walking at this point and could see a guy ahead dressed from head to toe in black, his lightweight rain coat hood pulled up over his head and his black race vest showing him to be part of the race. As I watched, a Range Rover drove past him through a big puddle that it could have easily avoided, showering him in freezing spray. Poor bugger!

I wasn't far back and managed to catch up with the guy.

"That Range Rover wasn't very polite," I said from behind, trying to strike up a bit of conversation. It was gloomy, raining and miserable, and a bit of banter would help pass the time.

"Sorry?" the guy said, half turning round.

"I said the Range Rover was a bit of a git."

He shook his head, signalling that he still couldn't hear me. We gave up trying to have a conversation and I dropped back a little, carrying on the trudge up the hill in the rain.

A car was coming down the hill as I was passing a rather hefty looking puddle, and it reached me just as another car passed in the other direction. There was no way for my car to avoid the puddle, and so now it was my turn to get soaked. Again. Fucking marvellous. This day was getting better by the minute.

I was soaking wet, and it was raining. I was freezing cold, and there was no life or joy in the sky or the general environment. I started pondering the idea of giving up at checkpoint 3. This "poxy little 45-miler" had given me a damn good kicking. I was going ridiculously slowly now – it was going to take forever to get to the end. Even if I could have unzipped my vest pocket to look at my timing chart I wouldn't have bothered as I knew I was a long way behind my target.

In a mood as gloomy as the weather, I turned left onto Ruffet Road which went slightly downhill. I really should have been running, but it felt like so much hard work with my feet in the state they were. I was becoming distracted by the pain that was now building back up in my hands from the cold too.

I tried to perk myself up a bit; there was no point in wallowing in a pit of despair as that wasn't going to get me to the end any quicker. And the end was where I was going to get, not checkpoint 3. I was on a road, not in a field. I was on flat terrain, and I knew where I was going. I was making progress. Things weren't all that bad, were they?

After a bit of meandering down a few more roads, I came to the main A342 and, as luck would have it, there were no cars coming so I crossed to the other side and tried my best to run along the pavement in the rain. I just about managed it and soon came to a left turn where a bunch of people were gathered, several sporting umbrellas, and others clapping and cheering, which is always a nice sight.

"This is *disgusting*," I shouted, and got a sea of confused faces looking back at me. Maybe I was too far away, given the road noise? Or maybe they thought I'd said something else. "It's really hard work!" I tried again, and this got more of the expected response, a few people saying well done, and the old classic "not far to go now." That's more like it!

I passed the people and continued the turn around to the left onto the start of a steep hill. I remembered this bit – a bit of a hill, then a turn to the left and a descent through some woods. There was a chap ahead of me quite a way up the hill, and after a minute or two I thought that maybe he'd missed the turn as I didn't remember it being this far up. But a little way further on, just past the first house on the hill, he disappeared from view.

I knew the descent was going to be a bit sketchy, so I'd already faffed around extracting my poles and clipping them back together before I reached the turn. As expected, there were plenty of slippery tree roots and a few wooden steps on the steep narrow woodland path, and the poles came in very handy.

For some reason, I thought the bottom of this hill ejected me onto a golf course, but it turns out I was wrong. Instead, I ended up on what looked like a farm track that gently descended into the wide-open view ahead. To the right was a raised embankment, and as I ran along the stony road a train went past along the top, the comforting sound momentarily making me dream of being sat in a comfy seat inside a nice, warm carriage.

I tried to make the most of the gentle downhill gradient of the road, and before long I found myself as far along as I was supposed to go before turning to the left through a gate onto the Frome Valley Walkway.

Then all hell broke loose.

# 8

*Balls deep in the Frome*

## Saturday 2nd March 2024, 13:22

On the other side of the gate was a narrow path that quickly turned to a set of wooden steps. I remembered this path being very muddy from previous times in this race but today it was on a new level. There was just a stream running down the path, creating a set of mini waterfalls down the steps, and there was no avoiding my feet going underwater.

When I reached the bottom, the path carried on next to the River Frome, and the water that had been running down the steps dissipated a bit leaving me on the expected muddy track. What I hadn't remembered was the mud turning to a nice, solid path, and I was beginning to think that what might have been a troublesome stretch was going to turn out to be relatively easy. Oh, how wrong I was!

Ahead, I could see the Frome, having turned sharply to the left, and I followed the line of the path, which led… into the water. I thought I must have it wrong, but the fence line which delineated the path to my left continued obliviously straight into the water.

Oh. Shit!

I stopped and looked back. There was no one behind. I looked ahead again, double checking that I wasn't about to make a huge mistake. My watch suggested I was still on the right route, and that fence running along next to the path sealed the deal for me, and so I headed forward into the water.

It went over my shoes, then past my ankles and up my shins. I put my poles out in front, feeling for any unexpected obstacles under the water and continued slowly. Now my knees were at the water level, and still it rose. The river rushed by to my right, fallen branches bobbing in the water as what I hoped was the bank as it was a fair distance away. The only point of reference for the path that I had was that fence, so I was following it, sticking just a short distance to the side.

When the water started making its way up my things, I found myself involuntarily breathing fast and hard, partly from the cold, and partly from the nervousness. But I was excited too – it's not every day you get to wade a river in an ultra!

The water made its way to the top of my things, causing me to gasp for obvious reasons. I was beginning to wonder just how deep it was going to get – would I have to take my pack off and hold it above my head? Would I be swimming soon?

After a minute or so of very, very slow movement, the level started to drop, and eventually the path seemed to lift back out of the water again. I breathed a massive sigh of relief, but I was also a little sad that the excitement was over.

I needn't have been, because it wasn't.

A little way ahead was what looked like a lake. The problem was, the path again disappeared underwater, but this time, there was no fence to follow. There was one person ahead making their way very slowly forward, and just beyond them were a couple of lone handrails poking above the water line. I assumed they were attached to a bridge, and that was where we should be heading.

I hoped like hell the path went in a straight line to the bridge otherwise I was likely to be going for an impromptu swim. I started ahead, again using my poles for obstacle detection. I stepped slightly around some branches poking up out the water hoping I wasn't straying too far from the path, the cold and murky red-brown water now back up to the top of my thighs again. It was very cold, but I was just concentrating on taking deep breaths and moving forward towards the bridge.

I reached the edge of the bridge and felt around with my foot under the water for the first step. I found it, and stepped up to the second step, then the third. There wasn't a fourth, so I figured I must be at the top now.

The guy in front yelled something back to me, but I couldn't hear him. It was said with some urgency, so I shouted for him to repeat.

"There's a missing plank, watch out," he shouted loudly.

"Oh, bloody hell, thanks!" Nothing like a random hole in the ground to keep things even more interesting!

I shuffled my feet along the wood and found the missing bit; that could have been nasty, and I was very grateful for the guy who'd yelled back. I stepped over and continued on to the end of the level part of the hand rail, then felt back out for the steps down and got back onto what I assumed was the underwater path now that I was back to being balls deep in the Frome.

There was a line of 3 or 4 people spaced out ahead, so I could see the route to take now and I relaxed a bit, knowing it was at least possible. The guy in front was videoing with his phone, and I wished I could have got mine out to capture this surrealist of ultramarathon moments, but there was no way my hands would be able to unzip the pocket, and even if they could, I was certain my phone would end up in the Frome.

Eventually, the water started to subside, and I found myself back on a muddy path that undulated through woods and over tree roots. Out of the water, my legs felt numb and strangely warm, but my overriding feeling was relief. Unlike after the first submersion, I had now decided that enough was enough, so was slightly worried when the water level started rising again, but it was a short spell and I soon ended up on a road. If I wasn't dripping wet, I wouldn't have believed that had just happened!

I knew roughly where I was here, crossed Dingle Bridge and turned into the quaintly named lane called The Dingle. Despite being dunked in the water moments before, I now felt no worse than any other time during the day. Everything drained well, and my shoes and socks felt no wetter than after traversing the many wet fields. My hands, however, hated me. The pain in my fingers was pulsing in time with my heartbeat, and I couldn't wait to get to the checkpoint and try and do something about it.

I continued up The Dingle, knowing there was left turn coming up that would take me into the woods. I followed a guy ahead straight past the left turn into the woods, which was a silly thing to do considering what I'd just said. We both turned back at pretty much the same time and took the path which led us back down to the River Frome. Thankfully, here it hadn't breached the banks and crossing the bridge was easy.

The route was a wide woodland track covered in puddles which, considering how wet I'd just been, I didn't even bother trying to avoid. After not too long, I came out of the woods onto a road which I remembered not being too far from the checkpoint, but not too near either – maybe about a mile?

The obvious thing to do would have been to check the distance on my watch, but despite trying a few times, I couldn't get my thumb to press the button on the watch to change from the map screen. The muscles in my hand and wrist were so cold, they just couldn't create enough pressure, so I gave up. Knowing how far the checkpoint was wouldn't change how far away it was, so I told myself to just keep taking steps and I'd arrive soon. Fifteen minutes tops.

I followed the route on my watch, a few turns here and there, all on road. I reached a gate where a bunch of people were gathered, clapping and cheering. Climbing the big gate would have been the quickest and cleanest way forward, but there was no way I could do it with my hands. Instead, I had to go through two wooden gates to the side, using my wrist to push the levers, and then through one of those horse-trough things composed of two planks of wood, this one filled with water like a lovely little muddy footbath.

As I turned the corner, the little flag indicator showed at the bottom of the screen of my watch meaning that the checkpoint was now straight ahead – no more turns.

The road got busier, people were clapping, shouting encouragement and then guiding me to the left through the garden of White Horse pub and into the big gazebo that had been set up as the checkpoint.

I collapsed into a chair, put my head forward and closed my eyes, thankful that I'd made it but just wanting a moment to sort my head out before I tackled what needed to be done.

# 9

*So frustrating!*

## Saturday 2nd March 2024, 13:48

| CP3: Hambrook | |
|---|---|
| Distance (from previous) | 28.6 (12.2) miles |
| Time (from previous) | 1:48 pm (2h 45m) |
| Target Time | 1:00 pm (-48 mins) |
| Elevation (from previous) | 2,929ft/893m (1040ft/317m) |
| Time at Checkpoint | 31 minutes |
| Competitors Remaining | 169 |

In previous years the checkpoint had been in the car park of the pub, so the gazebo was an unexpected surprise which gave me an opportunity to sit down somewhere a little warmer than right out in the open.

I had been hoping for a hot drink here, but when I finally got to lifting my head back up and taking a look around, I couldn't see anything resembling a kettle, urn or other hot drinks dispenser. I stood up, still completely kitted out for the race, and went over to the food table. I clumsily picked up a peanut butter sandwich, a cheese sandwich and 4 or 5 chocolate digestive biscuits and went back to the seat.

After munching the two sandwiches and a couple of the biscuits, I had a go at getting my pack off. The Salomon pack has tension strings across the front which hook into a little plastic gripper on the other side of the vest. It's relatively easy to clip together and unclip, *if* you can use your hands. I spent about 2 minutes working away at one of the clips, trying all sorts of pushing movements with my completely numb fingers, eventually figuring out that I could hook a couple behind the string and pull hard in a certain direction to release the clasp. Having undone the pack, I shuffled it off my back and dumped it unceremoniously on the floor.

Next step was to try and get my gloves off. Wet material against my fingers was going to keep them cold, so counterintuitively, I needed to get the gloves off to warm my fingers up. And now I was back to the problem of having absolutely no ability to grip! Have you ever woken up in the night having fallen asleep on your arm, and then tried to do anything with your hand when it's numb and tingling? That's the sort of situation I was in. I tried to grab the ends of the fingers with one hand but just couldn't get enough force behind it to pull the material.

Luckily, another runner saw what I was up to and came over to help. She also suffered from Raynaud's but had been more sensible than me as she still seemed to have use of her hands. She gently grabbed the ends of the gloves, and a moment later, my hands were out in the open. They weren't a pretty sight – a patchwork of purple, blue and red spotted skin, the fingers entirely white like those of a corpse. All part of the fun of an ultramarathon though, eh?

I sat in the chair shivering, knowing I had a lot to do but also that nothing was going to get done until I got the function in my hands back. While waiting, I figured I should eat some more, so I stabbed at the digestives on the floor and managed to grip them and get them up into my mouth.

The zip on the back of the pack didn't need much work to open, and I soon had a drybag out and sat on my lap. Try as I might, I again couldn't summon enough squeeze in my fingers to open the clip, so I asked the guy sat beside me who kindly obliged. I got out my warm hat that didn't have a peak, but did cover my ears, and pulled out a pair of waterproof gloves. I had this idea that my hands were so cold not because they were wet, but because they *kept* getting wet and I repeatedly drained all the heat from them. If I put my squeezed-out, damp gloves back on and covered them with a waterproof layer, the heat would hopefully stay inside, and my hands should warm up. That was the theory, anyway. And to be honest, I had no other tricks up my sleeve.

I dumped the hat and gloves on the floor for later, clipped up the drybag (I could push the clips together, but not squeeze them apart), and put it back in my pack. Next, out came the emergency drybag which I'd never intended to open. Again, I asked the guy next to me to open it and pulled out my lightweight fleece. My coat came off and the fleece went on, with me doing a pretty decent impression of a toddler trying to get a jumper on themselves for the first time. With my coat back on, I was still shivering, but I hoped that I would start to warm up now.

I closed the drybag and put it back in my pack, frustrated that everything was taking so much longer that it should have. I knew the only real way I was going to warm up was to get moving again, but I still had a lot to do.

I ran through my mental checklist and the next item was water. I couldn't unscrew the tops of the bottles, but I had help from someone at the table and the bottles were soon filled again.

My Jabra headphones came out next, and I slowly took them out the waterproof bag, opened the case, fumbled one earbud into my right ear, closed the case and put it away. It should have taken 15 seconds, but it took closer to 2 minutes. This was *so frustrating!*

I found my packet of paracetamol and managed to bite two of them out of the pack – there was no way I could push them out. I swigged some water to get them down.

The overriding thought at this point was that I must never, ever, *ever* let my hands get this cold again. From now on, I would always stay on the warm side of comfortable, and I would make damn sure I had extra layers with me. This was an incredibly annoying situation to be in and, worse still, it felt like with a bit more care I could have avoided it.

I got my phone out and after a very frustrating couple of minutes I had the live set list from the Bring Me the Horizon concert I'd gone to with my son back in January. I hit the repeat button so I wouldn't have to get my phone out again, pressed play and set the volume to something that seemed sensible.

Nearly there.

I put my pack back on, but despite having been in the gazebo for almost half an hour now, I still couldn't get my fingers to work enough to clip up the vest. Luckily, a lovely lady who was waiting for her husband to come in helped, and she managed to get both my water bottles back in the vest too.

Last thing – gloves. I stuck my claws into the gloves and spent ages pulling them down, trying to guide my fingers into the holes. I kept getting them wrong, having to pull the glove back up and try again, but eventually got them over my hands. Not all fingers were in the right place, but it would do for now – if… *when* my fingers warmed up, I could sort them out. I pulled the yellow Salomon waterproof mitts over the top, and that was me done.

Music, paracetamol, fleece, gloves, water, food. My stop in the checkpoint should have taken 5 minutes; it took over 30. But I was now finally ready to get going.

I felt a lot more wrapped up when I left the pub garden and got back onto the road. I wasn't warm, but there was potential there. Several people clapped and told me I was doing great as I made my way up the road to the junction ahead. I didn't feel like I was doing great. I thought I was doing particularly poorly today.

I picked up to a fast walk heading up Bristol Road, enjoying the fact that I had enough feeling in my feet to be confident of my footing. My feet were still cold, but the pain had mostly subsided, and they were starting to feel vaguely normal again.

The M4 motorway loomed overhead momentarily, each carriageway perched atop angled concrete stilts and blocking out the light from the sky for a moment – not that I really noticed, as the dull, grey sky wasn't producing much light of its own.

I followed the path of the runner ahead around a corner to the right, then a left at St Elizabeth's Hall. I picked up to a run, the food and rest from checkpoint 3 now starting to give me a bit of energy and overtook the runner ahead of me, which was a nice boost. I had been the one being overtaken for the last few hours, and it was nice to be feeling like I was making good progress.

I ran past houses, trees, and then over the M32 – there are a lot of motorways around Bristol! As I descending down the other side of the bridge, the path became a narrow strip on the grass verge, and I found myself with another runner within sight a bit of a way ahead. He seemed to veer out into the road for some reason, then head back onto the verge. When I arrived at the same spot outside a construction site, I could see why – a massive puddle filled with brown water half blocked the road. Luckily, it was a quiet road, and I could mirror his path and keep my feet from getting soaked for the umpteenth time today.

The music in my ear was a nice addition, giving a background tune to the afternoon. I wasn't paying a huge amount of attention to it, but one line in the song *AmEN!* caught my ear:

"Just let me suffer / Just let me breathe / Just let me suffer / Suffer in peace".

I felt like I has been suffering, and I wasn't out of the woods yet, but on the whole, things were definitely moving in the right direction. My feet were working. My hands were some way behind, cold but no longer painful, just tingling with that feeling of life slowly returning – those waterproof mitts were doing a good job of keeping the heat in.

At the end of the road, I came to the main Stoke Gifford Bypass road at the same time as the guy that had been in front of me. It was a busy road, but as we'd arrived at a crossing there were gaps in the traffic, so we both waited for a moment for one to come along. I noticed with interest that he had on a pair of Vivobarefoot shoes – I'm quite a fan of barefoot shoes and have mostly worn Merrell Vapor Gloves as my everyday (non-running) shoe but had bought a first pair of (ridiculously expensive!) Vivobarefoot shoes in London the previous month. I liked them a lot, but I'm not sure I'd want to do an ultra with such little protection on the bottom of my feet, despite being a pretty seasoned user of them.

We got across the road, and I continued ahead, enjoying the fact that – so far – there hadn't been any mud since the checkpoint. The rain had stopped, and my fleece was keeping my upper body nice and warm without being too hot.

I've run (well, started) the Arc of Attrition 4 times. It's a 100-mile race on the coast path of Cornwall in January, and the expectation is that you'll have foul weather – cold, wet, windy, potentially dangerous conditions that you need to prepare carefully for. In the four times I've run it, the weather has honestly never been as bad as this little jog around Bristol. I had learnt a lesson today – every ultramarathon needs to be taken seriously. And I needed to stop being an overconfident idiot. The Green Man might be at the shorter end of the races I typically do and all in the daylight, but the terrain is surprisingly tough, and it's plenty long enough for things to go very wrong indeed. Thankfully, it looked like I'd managed to sort myself out in the nick of time.

I turned right onto a bridge that crossed the railway line, although it wasn't immediately obvious as the sides of the bridge were quite high solid concrete. Yellow signs along the bridge warned 'Danger: Live wires below', which confused me initially. I live in an area where all the electric trains are powered by a third rail, but here, they were powered by overhead cables. I'd never thought before about how the bridges would have to be both high enough and protected to stop anyone being able to get anywhere near those cables. On the far side of the bridge was a line of metal fencing with gaps to see through, and I looked back to see the catenary gantry just beside the bridge, the 25,000-volt wire snaking along below.

I ran slowly along the quiet split pedestrian/cycle path that cut through the houses of Stoke Gifford, crossing an empty road that went past the entrance to Great Western Court which looked like some kind of business park. I continued along the tarmac path that ran within a row of trees and passed a guy with massive headphones on his head who was so captivated by whatever was going into his ears that he was oblivious to the real world and jumped as I shuffled past him.

The path ended at a road, and following my watch I took a right turn, then a left turn and ended up on a long straight road that I recognised and remembered having a busy main road to cross at the far end. A little way ahead were a couple of guys running together, and as I made my way along the road, the gap between us shrank.

They got to the main B4057 before me and pressed the button on the pedestrian crossing. It didn't take long for the lights to change, but I'd closed the distance to the point where if I ran fast, I could get across. So that's what I did, and it felt both wonderful and horrible at the same time!

I dropped back to catch my breath, and a gap built up again as I made my way through a brown housing estate. I was slightly confused by the route on my watch, but I seemed to be closing in on about 4 or 5 people in a dispersed groups ahead which gave me a target to follow. After a small stretch of yellow pathway and another road crossing, the track ran close to Stoke Brook and faded back into mud somewhere between Little Stoke and Bradley Stoke for the first time in the 25 minutes since checkpoint 3.

The group of us picked our way through the thickening mud under tree cover, trying to avoid the puddles captured between the big roots. My poles were packed away in my pack as there has been a lot of road up to now, and they kept catching on tree branches, meaning I was having to duck low a lot of the time which my legs were starting to seriously object to. The poles would have been useful as my feet were slipping and sliding around, but I was almost definite that by the time I got them out, I'd be back on solid ground. I hoped my memory was right.

A few minutes later, we turned onto a light-yellow solid stone path that went under a bridge that carried Bradley Stoke Way. I had caught up with a couple of guys and we got chatting. They mentioned they were from Aylesbury, so I told them I used to live near there, in a place called Hawkslade Farm which they knew well. It's funny how you run an ultramarathon 100 miles from your home, and bump into people from 100 miles away in a different direction, and it turns out you've both lived practically next to each other!

One of the Buck's chaps had a little fluffy duck in the stretch pocket on the back of his race vest, and I had to ask him about it.

"My son gave it to me. He wanted me to have something to give me good luck on the run." That brought a big smile to my face, what a lovely thought!

We carried on together as a group of 3, running along a little slower than I would have done had I been on my own, but keeping going for longer. I've mentioned this same scenario a few times now, and I think maybe I should try to slow down my running a bit when I'm tired and keep it going, rather than keep stopping to walk and then picking up a faster pace again. I'm not sure which is best, but it's worth trying both.

The track on my watch looked confusing ahead, a squiggle seemingly going in 3 different directions with no obvious view of what to do. When we reached the junction and could actually see the layout, it was easy – a little turn to the right to join a bridge, then back to the left across Bradley Stoke Way and then onto some particularly unmemorable roads until we came to the busy A38.

This road was a dual carriageway, with two lanes, then a central barrier, and 2 more lanes. There was no pedestrian crossing at the point we met the road, and the central barrier looked uncomfortably high to jump across, but a fair way down to the left there did look to be a gap in the barrier, and I had memories of crossing there before.

We started off in that direction, but one of the Buck's guys noticed the entrance to a subway which I'd somehow never spotted before. We headed down the steps, under the road and popped up the other side with little drama. On inspection of the official GPX, that *is* the correct route, and totally obvious now!

At the end of the next road, we skirted the edge of Aztec West Business Park, passing a large and impressive looking metal-and-glass building to the left. Ten years before, when I was about 34 miles into my very first ultra at this same spot, I was running with Sharon Sullivan and Mark Evans, the latter having just removed a couple of mini pork pies from his pack to eat. My stomach rumbled at the thought – I would kill for a pork pie right now!

# 10

*I'd forgotten about this hill*

## Saturday 2nd March 2024, 15:17

On the whole, things were good now. I was vaguely warm, and feeling a million miles from the freezing, shivering and pain from just an hour earlier before. I had over 30 muddy miles in my legs, so I wasn't absolutely tip-top, but considering where I was and what I had left to do, things were looking okay.

All the pavement through the business park section was block paving, and as I plodded along, I got to wondering why. It had been the same 10 years before, so it was obviously hard wearing. The ground was free of the typical undulations that old block-paving seems to suffer from, at least locally to me. Maybe the ground was a bit more solid here, with fewer trees near the path? Who knows, but it gave me something to think about for a couple of minutes, taking my mind off the running.

We turned left and continued round a long sweeping right-hand curve, moving out on to the road to avoid a couple of people walking big dogs. I was back to mixing running and walking with my average about the same as the Buck's guys, so as a group we all turned off the solid ground, crossed a low stile and headed onto a soft trail on the edge of a square of grass.

Over the space of 300m, the path transformed through firm ground, to damp stones, to wet stones, then into the familiar quagmire – black mud, puddles, stones, tree roots and a gentle stream of water running down the middle, meaning there was no real way to avoid wet feet. I was beginning to wonder if the Community Forest Path was actually just clever marketing for a drainage ditch around Bristol. The trees grew up tall here, covering the path and making it gloomy. The area felt like the back of an industrial estate, and there was a progressively louder continuous traffic noise coming from somewhere ahead. All in all, it was a pretty grotty area.

As it was a long straight section, I could see people ahead and someone behind me. We were all spaced out at intervals, so there was no conversation any more, but I had Oli Sykes yelling in my ear for company, so I was happy. At least until we took a left turn to run parallel with the M5 motorway, at which point I could hear precisely sod all of my music, it being drowned out by the hundreds of cars passing by across the 6 lanes.

There was a short stretch of still muddy path with the M5 on the right side and the back of some allotments on the left, then I reached the bottom of the bridge that would take me over to Over.

It seems this is intended strictly as a pedestrian bridge, judging by the two massive concrete pipe sections standing upright, leaving a person-sized gap between the path and the steps. Even without a bike, it felt a bit claustrophobic getting through, and I was glad I hadn't eaten too many mince pies at Christmas. I climbed the two flights of steps to the top and made my way across to the other side. It was a hefty bridge –

lots of big thick pipes welded together to make the structure, a solid metal floor and railings to stop any accidental meetings with the traffic below.

I descended and made my way through the second concrete squeeze-gap onto a gravelly pathway that continued the downward trend at a rather steep angle. I contemplated getting my poles out for support, but despite the ground being wet, the right-hand side of the wide path down felt grippy. It ran beside a metal fence, and as I went down, I reached out and grabbed the fence to see if I could stop myself should I fall. Even with the mitts on over my gloves I found I could grip enough, so I kept my hand out close to the fence in case my feet decided to slip out from under me.

The path met a road, which I slowly ran along for a while, still people visible ahead of me but not seeming to get any closer now. One by one they disappeared and when I reached the spot, I took the left turn over a stile and back onto another muddy path.

There was a lot going on along this path – lots of tree roots to avoid, and muddy patches so thick that it was best to avoid those too. But the overhanging branches kept snagging my poles, and the spiky bushes coming from each side would catch on my vest. It took a fair amount of concentration to traverse the path without faceplanting or getting too snagged.

At the end, I climbed over a stile and stepped onto a quiet lane. Everyone ahead of me had disappeared, and my watch map said to continue straight ahead, but there wasn't anywhere to go! I was faced with a driveway into a house, and next to that, a white 5-bar wooden gate into what looked like the houses garden. And then I spotted it. Between the gate and the bush was a white wooden bar, and underneath, a small, flat plank of wood – a stile.

I crossed over, hoping I was on the right path, and ventured into what still felt very much like someone's garden. Passing a small wood store, I spotted a familiar sight – a stile surrounded by the now familiar, large, muddy puddle.

The open field ahead was covered in longer grass wet from the rain, and within seconds my feet were, yet again, soaked through. There were patches of mud and the ground was occasionally quite slippery, so as I went along, I got my poles out again.

The route was easy – just follow the people ahead. I looked behind, and saw a couple of people coming along, so we were back in a train again. I seemed to be slightly gaining on the people ahead, and those behind didn't seem to be getting any closer.

I came to the corner of a field where, on the other side, there was a left and a right turn and it wasn't immediately obvious, either from the view ahead or on my watch, which was the right way. I heard a gate clang shut to the right, and there was my answer. I followed on round through the gate, and when the route opened up again I could see a few people ahead.

The ground was annoying. The path was obvious – a brown, slippery, muddy line down the middle of the field. The rest of the field was tufty lumps of uneven ground, not the nicest thing to run over. I spent my time trying to find the sweet spot between the mud and the lumpy ground to either side, mostly failing.

After a few more fields, we came to the corner of a recreation area in Easter Compton. There was a skate park to the left and an open basketball court ahead which gave us a nice moment of respite on solid ground as we crossed.

I recognised the road at the entrance to the recreation area and crossed over into the narrow alleyway next to Easter Compton Village Hall. I ran along the alley as I didn't want to hold anyone up that was behind me, but I don't think anyone was close enough to be bothered either way. We were all slowing down now, the muddy miles beginning to take their toll on everyone.

Another field to cross, this one a little more groomed, and then I was heading through the churchyard of All Saints Church at Compton Greenfield. Last time I ran this race back in 2022, I'd been running through here with two young guys who were doing their first ultra. One had a speaker in his pack and was blasting out N.W.A. and Eminem. Although I was enjoying the music, I thought the language was a bit inappropriate when passing groups of families out for a walk in the sunshine! Today, however, there was no music. There were no families. There was no sunshine.

The route became quite complex, lots of twists and turns through nondescript fields. To be honest, that statement applies to most of the route, but here I didn't have a lot of reference points when heading through field after field. There was a little section of road that I didn't remember, then a turn into some woods and through a metal gate, and then a sudden memory – Spanorium Hill!

"I'd forgotten about this hill," I said to the two Buck's guys who I'd ended up running along with again. The running soon stopped when we met the muddy steps though.

It's not a big hill at only a couple of hundred feet high but after 37 miles it took it out of me. I tried to push on the way up, making use of my poles on the slippery ground, but kept getting lightheaded spells on the way up, usually a sign that I hadn't really been eating enough. Still, I got to the top in the end, now back on my own having dropped back, and stopped to look around. It was a nice view from up here, made better by the hints of something other than rainclouds in the sky. Was it my imagination, or was the sun trying to find a gap in the greyness to punch through?

Nothing really changed at the top, other than the gradient. It was just more grassy, muddy fields. At one point, I came to a stile, but next to it the post holding the barb wire fence was down. I figured it would be quicker and easier to just step across the gap rather than negotiate the stile but managed to catch my foot on the barb wire in the long grass. I stabbed one of my toes and would have gone flying if it wasn't for my poles.

"Don't do that!" I yelled back to the guy behind.

I came into a big field that I recognised, more from the state of the path on the edge than anything else. It was sloping, muddy, puddly and an absolute pain in the arse to run along. Next to the path was long grass carrying the morning's rain water on its leaves and hiding a multitude of lumps and bumps on the ground. I kept swapping between the path and the grass, trying to find the easiest route, but ended up decided that neither was any easier than the other.

The path I was on followed the edge of the field, but I saw someone that I assumed was a dog walker right in the middle. But was that a race vest? A look at my watch map showed the route heading diagonally across the middle, so I turned 45 degrees to the left and headed into the longer grass. My feet got absolutely soaked, and it wasn't easy going, stepping over what felt like a thousand mole hills. A glance behind showed a few people taking the same route across to what I knew was the exit of the field in the far corner.

The final gate led us out onto a narrow lane, and I was delighted. If my memory was right, that was the end of the grass and mud, at least until after the next checkpoint.

I picked up to a shuffling run along the narrow lane, avoiding the odd puddle. I followed instruction from my watch at a junction and soon found myself again crossing the M5 motorway. The road quality degraded, great cracks in the edges making way for big puddles, but thankfully it wasn't a busy road so the water was easy to avoid. It was downhill too, so I kept the run up until the bottom, at which point I could see the main road ahead and tried to keep up the pace until then. I passed Cribbs Sports and Social Club and ended up out on Station Road in Henbury.

I did a quick system check. My hands were warm. My feet were warm and didn't feel too wet, despite that last field giving them a good soaking. I was at a comfortable temperature, with nothing too hot or remotely as cold as it had been earlier. I was knackered, but that was to be expected this far along.

The first part of Station Road rises up to a bridge over the railway, and as I'd just been running a fair way, I took this as an opportunity to walk for a bit. Once over the hump, I took up running again, but it didn't last as long as I would have liked until I found myself back walking. Then I got passed by another guy in the race.

For the first time in the race, I wanted to get that place back. I started running again to see if I could close the distance down. As I went along, I could hear a repetitive noise that I couldn't place – a squeak, squeak, squeak noise. I get annoyed by noises when I don't know what they are, so I held onto each bottle as I ran, thinking maybe they were rubbing in my vest, but no, it kept going. I tried holding various other parts of my pack, but the noise stayed.

I lifted the ear covers of my hat to get a better sense of where sound was coming from to try and pinpoint the noise. I still had one headphone in, so it wasn't going to be perfect, but I was starting to suspect my shoes. Maybe they were saturated with water and squeaking their objection. I slowed a little, but strangely, the tempo of the noise stayed the same. So, I stopped, and I heard it continue, getting slowly quieter. Then it clicked – it was the guy in front of me!

Happy to have figured out the source of the noise, I decided I'd had enough of running for now and the bloke ahead could have that place for now.

I was walking along one of those split pedestrian and cycle paths – the kind where one side is marked with a bike symbol and the other with a person. I'm a bit anal about sticking to the correct side; after all, if I were cycling, I'd be really annoyed if pedestrians were wandering all over the bike lane. Lucky for me, I was in the right place when a cyclist came zooming past, only to slam on the brakes and swerve right across in front of me to head into a house. Classy move. Patience is clearly overrated, eh?

I'd lost sight of that bloke that had been running ahead, but despite me walking, he came back into view. I could see that he too had given up with running, but I was clearly gaining on him. I do a lot of walking training and have a decent pace, so usually when it comes down to walking later in ultramarathons, I tend to catch and overtake quite a few people. I wasn't sure if I'd be able to catch him before the checkpoint, but it was a nice target to keep the motivation up.

I rounded a corner to the right, knowing the checkpoint wasn't far away. I checked on my watch – delighted that my fingers now worked and I could press the buttons – and found it was a mere 0.3 miles away. I needed to cross to the other side of the road but could hear a roaring engine working hard to get up the hill, although I couldn't see anything still, and figured that it must be a slow, heavy vehicle. I chanced it and ran across the road, again managing to avoid getting splatted, and the truck that finally appeared seemed to take an age to get up to where I was.

I went through the wide entrance gap in the cobbled stone wall around the Blaise Castle Estate – I was now sniffing distance from the checkpoint.

I started wondering about Blaise Castle – what exactly was it, and where did the name *Blaise* come from? As I was pondering this, I rounded the corner and saw a big building to my left which reminded me of follies local to me like Durlston Castle, so I assumed it must be the castle, not realising it was actually Blaise Mansion.

Hiding in the trees on the far side of the 650-acre parkland estate lies Blaise Castle, an 18th century Gothic Revival styled folly commissioned by Thomas Farr. It was built in 1766 on the site of chapel dedicated to Saint Blaise, a 3rd century bishop known for his miraculous healings - and hence the name of the whole estate, which houses not only the castle and the mansion I just passed, but also a hamlet of a few houses and now a museum within the mansion. Oh, and checkpoint 4 of the Green Man Ultra.

I passed an old couple that seemed to be talking together about what all these people were doing. They didn't seem like crew – just curious about why their day had been gate-crashed by a bunch of tired looking, muddy, sweaty runner types.

I came to a big puddle the took up the whole of the wide path ahead and, for once, I fancied not getting my feet soaked just before the checkpoint so opted to take the route through what looked like fairly shallow mud to the side. As I was tottering along the mud, I heard a splashing as the guy who had been behind me just ploughed straight through the middle – my usual tactic.

On hearing this noise, the guy just ahead of us started running. It seems like a little race was on to the checkpoint! I thought it would be rude not to join in, so the 3 of us ran at a pretty much identical slow pace along the remaining short stretch of tarmac path next to the wide-open grassy expanse of Blaise Park. We all turned right by the small crowd of clapping people, had our numbers taken and headed on towards the little kiosk at the end of the path.

# 11

*The iconic landmark in Bristol*

## Saturday 2nd March 2024, 16:36

| CP4: Blaise | |
|---|---|
| Distance (from previous) | 39.3 (10.7) miles |
| Time (from previous) | 4:36 pm (2h 48m) |
| Target Time | 3:14 pm (-82 mins) |
| Elevation (from previous) | 3742ft/626m (813ft/626m) |
| Time at Checkpoint | 3 minutes |
| Competitors Remaining | 155 |

The lady who had helped me fasten up my race vest and load up my bottles at checkpoint 3 was waiting here as her husband seemed to be running at about the same pace as me. She gave me a big smile and we said hello, then I thanked her again for helping back when I was freezing cold and let her know things were much, much better now! She had a tray of homemade ginger cake covered in icing which she offered me, and I thoroughly enjoyed a piece.

I filled up one of my soft flasks from a water bottle on the table. I didn't bother with the other as it was half full and there was only a little over 6 miles to go according to my watch. I saw a runner waiting with a cup of something hot in hand, so went up to the kiosk and asked if I could get a coffee. I offered my collapsible cup – this is officially a cup-less race after all – but we both decided that it wouldn't be very good for a hot drink. I went away with a cardboard cup, having completely forgotten about the other plastic cup buried in my pack which I'd carried around for the last 40 miles!

I deliberately asked for only half a cup of water in the coffee and back at the table I tried to top up with cold water so I could drink it quickly. I somehow managed to catch the water bottle on my glove and spilling some of the coffee over the table – idiot! I cleaned up then headed back the way I had come with my warm coffee, swigging as fast as I could as I walked back out towards the park. After saying thanks to everyone, I took a final big swig of the drink as I passed a bin, burning my throat in the process, then dumped the cup and got on with the last chunk of this race.

I headed off diagonally across the park, running with a guy that I'd been swapping places with for a while. For a change, the grass wasn't overly muddy; it was bordering on pleasant running across towards the back of the park. The sky seemed to be lightening, adding a tiny bit of much needed cheer to the days weather. The route on my watch continued onto a muddier section which still wasn't anything like the previous terrain, but I spotted a path into the trees that looked a lot firmer so headed over in that direction. The other guy I was running with obviously thought I knew what I was doing and followed along.

It was a nice, firm path, although it was going up which was slightly less pleasant than not going up. What was also becoming apparent the more I went along the path was that it was curving round in completely the wrong direction, and my track was starting to deviate significantly from the race route on my watch.

The path had led upwards a fair bit, with a steep drop on the side that I would need to get down to be back on the route, so it was looking like the only option was to go back the way I'd come and correct the mistake at the point I'd detoured. But part way back, I spotted a way down onto the grass that looked like it would be just about doable with my legs in the state they were, and I was soon back on the muddy grass below. Moments later, I was heading uphill again, but this time on the correct path. My attempt at a shortcut has added a little distance and a little hill. I reminded myself that I should stop trying to be clever – navigation was *not* my strong point!

The woodland path among the trees was firm and pleasant but was consistently going up, which was wearing me out. There were a set of steps at the top, and when I finally crested the summit, I was feeling quite exhausted.

Through a gap in the trees, I caught sight of something that I didn't think I'd be seeing today – the sun! It's typical, though – it doesn't show up all day, and then when it does, it's right in my face, blinding me! Still, it was nice to get a little heat and light from the big ball of fire to cheer us all up for a bit.

The sun shone down on the grass covered ridge of Kings Weston Hill that formed the next mile of our route, and we joined it next to the iron age Kings Weston Hillfort. The sun was shining right at me and I could see the silhouettes of runners ahead. I had the energy to run along at what felt like a slow pace, but I found myself catching up with and overtaking a few people. As I ran along, I reminisced about being here in the dark with Chris Edmonds, Sharon Sullivan and Mark

Evans all the way back in 2014 when I finished my first ultramarathon in just shy of 11-and-a-half hours.

My watch had shown a turn in 1 mile at the point I started along the ridge and I thought I'd be off into town quickly, but it seemed to take a long time to reach the end. The route turned a little to the left and I passed all 164 feet of the Kingsweston Aerial Mast, rising up high from behind the bushes and trees, and then I was descending towards the road.

Had I passed here just a couple of months later, I would have continued over the road on Kingsweston Iron Bridge. Built in 1821, the bridge crossed the Kings Weston Road until 2015, when a bloody great lorry clouted it, doing enough damage for the bridge to be closed. After a long running campaign by a group inventively called "Save the Iron Bridge", the repaired structure was craned into a slightly higher position at the end of April and re-opened to the public in July. I think competitors in the 2025 Green Man Ultra[3] will be making use of the reinstalled bridge her, but for me in 2024, as in 2022 and 2017, I found myself down on the northern side of Kings Weston Road and then crossing over a busy junction to join the top of yet another course at Shirehampton Golf Club.

The route was easy here, and I remembered it from previous years. All I had to do was stick to the left side of the steep grassy slope ahead, and run down past all the bunkers, greens and fairways. The ground was in good condition and grippy so from that point of view, the descent was pretty simple. But my quads were shot after 41 miles of muddy ground, so my pace down the hill was slow. All the time, I was thinking about the big, long climb I had to do soon, wondering why someone

---

[3] Of which I am one, and I shall be looking forward to seeing this bridge!

couldn't just fill in this big dip with a few trillion tons of rubble, giving me a nice flat bit of ground to run over.

I got to the bottom of the hill without stopping, crossed the busy road ahead when a gap presented itself, and continued on down a small set of steps that led onto an urban woodland path. It could have been a nice area, but seemed to have been commandeered as a dumping area for rubbish, with everything from McDonalds cups to a small fridge nestled in the undergrowth.

A few competitors were making their way towards a wooden stile was ahead, and there was a chap waiting to one side. I assumed he'd stood aside to let them pass over the stile, but then I noticed various tools hanging from tree branches – secateurs, shears and a serious looking if a little dirty blade poking out from a bit of wood. After dismissing him as a murderer (the obvious first thought), I concluded that he was here pruning back the trees.

"Watch out for the sharp things," he said in a proper Bristol accent, as the woman in front of me was struggling over the stile. It was my turn next, and I just stepped over without any issue, which I put down to the stairgate we used to stop the puppy from falling down the stairs. I could never be bothered to open it, so quickly learnt to just step over, even when I had no hands free from carrying all sorts. Brilliant for hip flexibility – and it seems to linger on, as we recently got rid of the stairgate (much to my dismay, as it was a great little exercise!).

The path was a decent bit of ground to run along; it was drier, and there was much less fighting through mud to keep running, although my legs didn't really have much run left in them.

At the next road, I met up with a woman who was waiting to cross, and we got chatting. She had run the 30-mile Green Man the year before and was doing the 45-miler today. She felt pretty good too – she'd made the decision to walk on all the slippery, muddy bits and had watched everyone else run on ahead of her, only to overtake them all on the easier bits and to still have something left in her legs now. That sounded like a bloody good plan, and I was envious of her enthusiasm and ability to actually run!

We continued on together through a bit of a housing estate and past a roundabout called The Pentagon, presumably named after the 5 straight sides that ran between the junctions when you look at it from above.

It was a bit of a maze around here and I'd been keeping an eye on my watch, but my current running partner knew where she was going. We turned into a cul-de-sac which I instinctively thought was a mistake until I spotted the gap between two houses at the end which led onto a path, and onto across another mostly firm grassy area alongside the River Trym.

We took the road across the river, then continued straight ahead across another road and then began to climb, at which point my running turned into walking, albeit pretty fast walking. I was beginning to get that familiar feeling when I get close to the end of an ultra – a sort of energy, or I suppose more of a lack of worrying about what might go wrong if I push myself a bit hard.

My dropping to a fast walk had seen me lose my running partner only to then catch up with her again as she started walking, and after a couple of turns we found ourselves at the bottom of the alleyway that signalled the climb up toward

Clifton, nestled between a wooden fence and a big green bush. The climb to the top from here was only about 200 feet, but I'd built it up to be like climbing a mountain – I just wanted this last one over with.

The ground was rough and flinty, grippy and ideal for pushing on up the hill. I put my hands in my poles and explained that I was still okay walking and climbing and she'd no doubt catch up with me soon.

It started off well, almost like I really *did* have the energy to keep moving at the storming pace I was heading upwards at. The ground turned to tarmac, and I admired the old building that I was passing in an attempt to ignore the fact that I was starting to blow. The alleyway ended by opening out onto a wide road with no pavement, still climbing. I was slowing now, my breathing heavy, but still had some fumes in the tank to push on with – I was so close now!

Eventually, the gradient reduced, and I continued to walk on, my pace increasing as the ache in my legs dissipated. I heard the thud-thud-thud of running shoes behind me and turned back to see the woman I'd been running with and another guy coming along.

"Don't you know it's illegal to run up a hill?" I shouted back and got laughter in response. They came up alongside me, and I continued "I'm really trying to think of an excuse not to run, but nothing is coming to me!" As I finished the sentence, my feet picked up into a shuffle and I started running along with them. It was horrible!

The road levelled off, then came to a junction and we crossed straight over onto the green grass of The Downs. The other two ran on as I gave up with that nonsense and dropped back to a walk. I meandered around a bit on the grass initially as I wasn't quite sure which direction to head in, but the combination of my watch decided to behave itself and the runners ahead of me going in one obvious direction sorted it out.

I found myself in between two rows of trees obviously meant to be a thoroughfare across the grass but bringing with it the effect of many feet on the same bit of wet grass – namely, mud. There were big brown patches, some big puddles and the ground was occasionally a bit slippery, but none of this was a real impediment to running. What *was* an impediment to running was the fact that I didn't want to, because I was absolutely knackered. I'd run when I get to solid ground, I told myself, otherwise it's just a waste of effort. The other two running on ahead stayed slow and consistent, building up quite a gap, and making me envious of not having just put in a tiny bit more effort and kept up.

About three-quarters of the way along its length, I joined "Ladies Mile" – a road that runs in a dead straight line for a kilometre from Stoke Road next to Durdham Downs, across Clifton Down, curving towards the end to meet up with a couple of main roads. Ladies Mile is associated with a woman called Victoria Hughes who was a toilet attendant on Stoke Road from 1929 to 1962. She became well known for her caring, non-judgemental support of woman in the area, many of whom were sex workers. During this time, she kept notes of her encounters and, at the age of 80, published them in her memoir, "Ladies Mile" in 1977.

Another fun fact: I didn't know at the time, but just over 300 metres away on the edge of the grassy area to my left was a stone chimney-like structure – a ventilation shaft for the mile-long, 150-year-old railway tunnel that ran a couple of hundred feet pretty much directly under where I was now.

I kept to my word, despite still not wanting to, and picked up to a run along the last stretch of Ladies Mile It curved around to the left and met the road of Clifton Down, but adjacent to the road was a wide path dotted with pedestrians, the odd cyclist and, in the distance, one or two runners. Nothing stays flat for long in Bristol it seems, and I could see ahead that the pretty tree-lined path ahead climbed and kept climbing. It wasn't steep, but it didn't need to be right now – I wasn't going to be running this bit!

I fixated on those Green Man competitors ahead and tried to will myself to walk faster and catch them up. They disappeared into trees and so, in the end, I had no idea if I closed the gap at all, but it gave me something to think about as I climbed the hill. After the small patch of woodland, the space opened out and ahead lay the Avon Gorge. From my vantage point, there wasn't much visibility of the drop, but I could see trees on the far side, and hills in the distance. Off to the left was the stout building of Clifton Observatory.

All the way back in 1766, a windmill for grinding corn was built on a spot overlooking the Avon Gorge. Over the following 11 years, two fires broke out. The second gutted the building leaving it derelict until, in 1828, an artist named William West rented the site and transformed it into the observatory we see today. West installed a camera obscura in Clifton Tower, a device which projects a panoramic view of the surrounding area onto a circular table inside a darkened room. Remarkably, it's still there today, open to the public, and one of only three working camera obscuras left in the UK.

Nine years later, West completed a 200-foot-long tunnel leading to a cave beneath the observatory. At the end of the tunnel, you'll find St. Vincent's Cave (also known as Ghyston's Cave, named after one of the Bristol Giants), which opens onto the cliff face of the Avon Gorge some 250 feet above the river and 90 feet below where you started.

I've run the Green Man five times now, but I've never taken the time to explore Bristol. The city is full of fascinating sights, and I can't wait to return one day to spend time exploring places like the observatory, the suspension bridge, the various mine sites, and more.

The path split ahead of me, with my watch suggesting the left turn which would be the most direct route across the grass, but I ignored it and went straight ahead. I could see people gathered by a railing ahead, and I was pretty sure I knew why. When I reached the edge, I stopped and just took in the view for a moment.

On 8th December 1864, five years after the death of Isambard Kingdon Brunel, the Clifton Suspension Bridge finally opened almost 35 years after construction started, and over 100 years after the idea was first proposed. The bridge road deck is 100 metres above the water of the River Avon, and with a total length of over 400 metres and a span between the towers of over 200 metres, it's an impressive beast, made all the more so by its position perched atop the steep sides of the Avon Gorge.

Please indulge me in a minor diversion from the story of the race to waffle a little about this amazing bit of engineering…

Brunel was only 24 years old when he won the design competition for the bridge, and construction started in 1830 only to be halted after 4 months by the Bristol Riots. Nothing moved for a further 5 years, but the delay had caused funding issues, and progress stuttered. For most of the 1850s, just the two unfinished towers stood on either side of the gorge.

A narrow, 300-metre-long metal bar spanned the gorge, allowing the movement of construction materials and, incredibly, people. This setup, known as the *suspended traveller*, featured a basket car that hung from the bar and was pulled across using ropes and pulleys. Over its 17 years of use, there were instances where the basket got stuck or the ropes broke, which must have been terrifying, but fortunately, there were no major accidents.

Brunel died in 1859, sadly never getting to see the finished bridge, but the following year, things started moving again. First, there with a bit of a redesign by William Henry Barlow and Sir John Hawkshaw to improve the width, height and sturdiness of the deck, adding three sets of chains instead of two. Then the fortuitous demolition of Brunel's Hungerford suspension bridge over the Thames in London to make way for a new railway bridge to Charing Cross liberated an appropriate length of hefty chains, which were then used at Clifton, and finally in 1864, the bridge was opened.

It's an iconic - no, *the* iconic - landmark in Bristol, and has been a part of many significant events. There was the first "modern" bungee jump by a bunch of nutters from Oxford University Dangerous Sports Club (not a club I'd be joining!) in 1979. The last ever Concorde flight in 2003 ended an era as she flew over the bridge on approach to Filton Aerodrome, captured in so many photos of the beautiful plane above this beautiful bridge. And, taking a gruesome turn, in July 2024 the discovery of human remains in a couple of suitcases on the bridge led to the arrest of a Columbian national for the murder of two people.

Right, history lesson over – back to the story!

My hands were fully functional now, nothing like the useless stumps they had been back at checkpoint 3, so I dumped my poles down, got out my phone and took a few photos of the magical view.

As I was snapping away, an Irish woman in the race ran behind me and asked if I was okay. I was feeling great compared to earlier, but maybe I was looking haggard and ruined? Or maybe she just hadn't seen my phone and assumed I'd given up, leaning against a railing high above the Avon Gorge just a couple of miles from the end of the race. I assured her I was fine, took a final few photos and, as I was zipping my vest back up and starting to wander along the path, bumped into the guy I'd run across the grass at Blaise with.

Just next to the Clifton Observatory, a little way down from the top of the path we were on, a group was gathered making quite a lot of noise as they took it in turns to tackle the Ancient Stone Slider, a natural rock slide that's been worked smooth by the buttocks of countless thousand Bristolians and visitors alike! Sliding down would have actually taken us in the right direction, but with my legs in the state they were, would also likely end up requiring a trip to casualty, so we continued around on the zigzag path to the bottom and onto the B3129

– the road that crossed the Clifton Suspension Bridge. I was back on my own at this point momentarily, until I bumped back into the Irish woman who had checked I was okay earlier. She came from my left, obviously having taken a little unintended tour of the observatory grounds, ending up just ahead of me as we passed the back of the toll booth buildings and entered the bridge. Too late, I noticed the sign saying 'No Entry' – there was a one-way system and we were supposed to be on the other side, but there was now no way across the road!

I followed the Irish woman into the throng of people coming towards us, thinking this was going to be a disaster. But in the end, it actually worked out quite well – rather than getting stuck behind people who had no idea there was anyone behind them, we were running *at* people who, on the whole, got out of the way! Sadly, because I spent most of my time concentrating on not ploughing into anyone, I didn't have much of a chance to enjoy the view, and too soon I reached the far side.

I knew we had to be on the other side of the road, so slowed to check for a gap, but my running partner seemed not to care, running across between two admittedly slow cars, on a mission to get to the end of the race. Once across and on the pavement, I walked for a bit while she ran on into the distance.

I could see a few more people in the race ahead, slowly climbing the hill, and I tried to run a couple of times, but I just couldn't get going. I kept my walking pace as fast as possible up to the traffic lights at the top of the hill, and by the time I got there, the guy who I'd met up with briefly back at the observatory had caught up with me.

This final road to cross was a busy one with fast moving traffic, although there was a pedestrian crossing with a set of lights. Both of us stood, eyeing the traffic and waiting for a gap, not even bothering to press the button. Eventually, we took our chance, racing across to the far side then up to and through the gate house into Ashton Court.

The nice, flat tarmac road stretched on in front of us, but where would the fun be in any more solid ground? Instead, we turned immediately left into the Red Deer Park and found ourselves back on familiar mud and grass. Although it was only a mile to the finish, I knew a fair chunk of it was downhill and potentially slippery, so it seemed sensible to ask my poles for one last bit of help.

Tucked in the corner of Ashton Court, on a small hill near an oak tree, is the Green Man – or rather, his head, intricately carved from stone. His pointy nose and eyes gaze towards the race finish line, while one side of his face is adorned with branches and leaves. In place since at least 2007, the sculpture was originally a bright cream stone but has now weathered to a fittingly green hue. He sits quietly and unassumingly, watching on as the race competitors make their way to the finish, easy to miss if you don't know he's there.

We passed Mr Green Man, and I said that we ought to give him a wave, so we both did as we ran past. The level grass started to tilt downwards and, although I couldn't remember exactly how far or what was coming, I was pretty sure I could give it a bit of a blast.

"Less than a mile to go, I shouldn't blow up now," I said to the guy as I began to pick up pace.

"Go for it!" he replied, as I started opening my legs up a bit and trying to run quickly down the hill. It worked… sort of. I was staggering a bit, and if I'd trodden on anything too uneven, I would have gone flying, but I kept up a reasonable pace for at least 30 seconds until I started feeling dizzy. I didn't care through, there can't be much left, and it's not like I was going to pass out. Probably.

I rounded an unexpected corner and at the bottom of a slope I saw a group of 3 or 4 people laughing, swearing and tottering very slowly around a fair amount of mud on the path. I slowed down a bit, but not much, and figured if I stuck to the grass and used my poles then… well, I didn't really know, but I didn't have a better plan as braking hard wasn't going to happen with my legs or this mud.

I almost ended up in a heap on the grass but managed to catch the trip, then continued to run down past the group, using the upward slope next to them to drop my pace a bit. I apologised as I came past like the out-of-control idiot that I was!

Ahead, I saw the car park for Ashton Court Mansion. I was pretty sure the route went through the car park, but as I came to the entrance I couldn't turn in time, overshot and ended up on a patch of grass on the far side. I dropped down onto a road that ran just below the car park and, annoyingly, climbed up a little hill that would have been avoided had I taken the right route. To my right on the other side of the dark metal fence that was a familiar site around Ashton Court, I could see people on the grass below. At the end of the short road – where it met with the back end of the car park – was a gate onto the grass which I took and then continued my downhill effort which was beginning to seriously run out of steam.

I tried to keep the running up, using my poles to keep me upright. I needed something else, so I rewound my playlist by 2 tracks. Whoever decided that a triple-click of a headphone button was a good idea to go to the previous track is a bloody idiot – it's difficult enough when you're stationary, but when trying to run downhill with knackered legs on slippery grass and a pair of poles, it's almost impossible! I managed it though, somehow, and *Artificial Suicide* by Bad Omens started up.

The drums kicked in, and Noah Sebastian started shouting at me, which gave me the boost I needed. I followed the GPS track in a straight line across to the gate ahead, a guy lingering nearby looking suspiciously like a marshal.

"Well done," he said as I approached. "You can go through the gate or the mud," he offered, pointing at the options.

"Mud will do!" I shouted, not wanting to stop to negotiate the gate, and it wasn't like I was going to get any muddier than I already was!

Through the fence I entered the field where it had all started at 8 o'clock this morning. It was getting darker, with the sun having set about 10 minutes before, the orange and white flags flapped gently in the breeze forming a corridor to the finish line area which was bustling with activity.

I heard lot of cheering and clapping in the distance as I was approaching which spurred me on, but as I ran across the field the noise subsided, and I ran along between the flags to the finish line with no fanfare at all. It didn't bother me much; I was just delighted that I'd finally got to the end of what felt like a good contender for the hardest ultramarathon I've ever done.

# 12

*Forensic scientist mode*

## Saturday 2nd March 2024, 18:04

| Finish | |
|---|---|
| Distance (from previous) | 45.8 (6.5) miles |
| Time (from previous) | 6:04 pm (1h 28m) |
| Target Time | 4:30 pm (-94 mins) |
| Elevation (from previous) | 4,402ft/1,342m (660ft/201m) |
| Competitors Finishing | 155 |

My name was taken along with a note of the time, and I then wandered around aimlessly in that post-finish daze – a mix of tiredness and elation, and the wonderous joy of knowing that I didn't *have* to keep moving anymore.

After a minute or two, I remembered I was supposed to have a medal and asked someone about it who sent me over to Steve Worrallo, the race director, to pick one up. I tell you what, running the Green Man is worth it for the medal alone! It's consistently one of the nicest medals for any race, and it seems to get better every year.

There are 4 different medals, 1 for the 30-mile race, and 3 for the 45-mile race depending on your position. Mine was a "Top 100 Finisher" – a red background with the head of the

Green Man taking up the centre half, beautifully embossed and enamelled in green and black. A pewter coloured ring surrounds the head, and in a ring on the edge are the words *O' wind, if winter comes, can spring be far behind.*

The Top 50 medal is the same but black where mine is red, and with the words *In the depth of winter, I finally learned that within me there lay an invincible summer.* If you're in the top 150 finishers, the medal is blue with *No winter lasts forever, no spring skips its turn.* I'm not quite sure what the 5 people that came in places 151-155 this year got as a medal though.

The medal for the 30-mile race, also called the Green Boy, is a little smaller but otherwise very similar, and the inscription reads *I think that to one in sympathy with nature, each season in turn seems the loveliest.*

See what I mean about the race embracing the folklore?

There was no hot food available at the end, but there was a goody bag that we all got with sandwiches and a few other munchables in, so I enquired about that too.

"They're inside, go and grab one. Don't forget you'll need to take your shoes off." A-ha! Finally, I get to use those shoe covers that I've carried around for 45 miles!

Outside the school entrance, I dropped my bag from my back, put my single earbud away so I didn't lose it, then got out a pair of the shoe covers and went into forensic scientist mode. At least at the bottom of my legs, anyway.

Inside, I picked up a chicken and bacon sandwich, a Freddo chocolate bar, and a packet of Space Raiders which I haven't had for *years* and was really looking forward to! Walking back to the car with my loot, I passed a guy walking with no shoes on, which is what I would have done if I'd have to take them off. Instead, I was wandering along with bright blue booties on over my shoes, as I just couldn't be arsed to take them off.

Back at the car, I opened the boot and chucked in my poles and race vest, then decided I might as well try and put as much in there as I could now, before I seized up. Off came my shoes, a pair of socks, another pair of socks, gaiters and shorts, all into the boot on top of the plastic boot liner that I bought when I got the car and has saved the carpet from stinky, sweating running gear on many occasions.

My running tights were more of a pain to get off. They were so caked in mud that I had to pull them down a bit, then stand on one side in order to get enough traction to slide them down my legs. Into the boot they went. I still had my compression shorts on, and I wasn't going to strip in the car park, so that would do – I put my walking trousers on, fresh socks and loose shoes, and it felt bloody lovely!

I couldn't wait any longer for the sandwich, so I took some bites and put it on the seat of the car while I took off my coat and compression t-shirt, replacing them with a clean t-shirt and a jumper. I sat down in the car and sank into the seat, enjoying the rest as I finished off the sandwich, then the Space Raiders, then the Freddo. I still had plenty of the water left from the drive in the morning, so I had a good swig of that too.

I wasn't satiated. I hadn't eaten anything like enough on the run, and a sandwich and packet of crisps wasn't going to make up for 45 miles of plodding around Bristol. I fiddled around on Google Maps and found a Burger King that was on the route home into the car. At just before 6:30 pm, I got going.

A short drive and £16 later, I had a disappointing burger, fries, drink and cheese bites. Maybe I wasn't as in the mood as I thought I was, but I hadn't had a Burger King for years, and it didn't taste as nice as I remembered.

I took the drive home slowly. I was tired but still alert, and besides, it was vastly easier than the drive up in the morning as the roads were completely clear of snow, like it had never happened.

It seemed like a sensible idea to have a break half way home, and I'd already done some planning, so at 7:50 pm I found myself trying to work out the tariff on a ticket machine in a car park in Warminster. Having satisfied myself that parking was free, I followed the map on my phone to The Bath Arms, the Wetherspoons pub in town (obviously!).

I drove back out the car park 45 minutes later, one alcohol free beer and one roast chicken dinner heavier, all for significantly less than the cost of the Burger King. An hour after that, I was home.

Green Man number 5 – done!

# 13

*Epilogue*

Something wasn't right with me from about November 2023 through to July 2024. My Garmin kept telling me all my stats were awry – resting heart rate up, heart rate variability down, performance poor, recovery needs high.

It was one of those things that you notice when you've come *out* of it. During those months, I just thought that maybe it was natural decline, albeit suddenly a bit rapid. But 6 weeks after my failed attempt at the Jurassic Coast 105 race in June, I managed to run the first 40 miles of the race route 90 minutes faster – a huge improvement, and a feeling that things were starting to get back to normal. The only conclusion I can come to is that I had some kind of low-level, long-term virus that nabbed 10 or 20 percent of my energy.

I ballsed up another race in October (book coming, obviously!), but that was for different reasons; physical performance wasn't so much the issue in that one.

I'd like to think that my heavier breathing and slower time at the Green Man in 2024 was due to whatever was bothering my body over that time, although I do think a lack of focussed training and a bad attitude coming in (*this will be easy, it's only 45 miles and it's in March!*) didn't help. I've run quite a few ultras now, most of them more than double the distance of the Green Man, and I think it's fair to say that I got a bit complacent before this event.

I like to finish my books by reviewing the race and looking at things I could have done better – after all, that's part of the reason I write the books in the first place!

And so, without further ado, I present a few things I should try and learn from:

**Stay Warm!**

If you get too cold, it's difficult to recover from it. More specifically, keep your hands warm, because when they get so cold they don't work, you can't even try to fix the problem by adding more warm layers.

**Long Runs**

I didn't really do any long runs in the lead up to this race, and I think that was a bad idea – it turns out the old long un' is probably actually useful! I've heard podcasts where semi-elite people talk about lower-mileage weeks and took it all a bit too literally – a low mileage week when you're coming down from 100+ miles per week is still a lot of miles, rather than dropping down my mere 40-50 miles per week even further. I'm going to try and aim for 50 miles per week over at least 6 weeks before an ultra and aim for a 15-20 miler each week.

**Other Bits**

I didn't ache at all on Monday, and I wonder if that's because I didn't really push all that hard on Saturday? As I've mentioned above, my breathing wasn't right, my effort levels felt higher than they should have, and I think maybe that meant that I didn't really push my legs too hard. I'm not sure what the lesson is here – maybe that, assuming you're not feeling ill – make sure you keep pushing in the race, don't slack off.

My poles were surprisingly useful. My expectation had been that I wouldn't use them, but I think I must have had them in my hands for more than half of the race. For the sake of 300 grams, I think I'll stick them in my pack for next time, unless the weather is looking much better.

The woman I ran with towards Clifton Downs had mentioned that she walked the muddy bits, and had energy left towards the end - she didn't push too hard on the slippery terrain and could reap the reward later. Initially I thought this was a great idea, but I'm in two minds now.

I certainly don't think it's worth trying to run fast on super-slippery mud – you'll do nothing more than throw all your energy away. But to make progress in the race, you've got to be pushing at times you don't want to and, as you've read, the Green Man has quite a bit of mud usually! I'll keep it in mind next time I run the race, though.

So, there you go – the tale of the Green Man Ultra in 2024. I hope you've enjoyed the story; it's been a lot of fun to write, and I'm really excited to get back out in the mud in March 2025. I'll probably completely forget all the lessons I've written above but, hopefully, I'll get to give a little appreciative nod to the Green Man of Ashton Court before the sun sets.

# THE END

**Before you go…**

I genuinely hope you've enjoyed this book. If you did and have a few minutes to spare, I would be so grateful if you could leave a review (hopefully positive!) on Amazon, and maybe rave about how amazing it was to spend a few hours getting lost in these pages to all your friends on social media!

You can stay in touch over at:

[www.swcpplod.co.uk](www.swcpplod.co.uk)

and if you've got any questions or feedback, you can use the contact form or social media links on the site.

Thanks again for taking the time to read my book!

Printed in Great Britain
by Amazon